A LITURGY *of* GRIEF

A Pastoral Commentary on Lamentations

Leslie C. Allen

Baker Academic

a division of Baker Publishing Group
Grand Rapids, Michigan

© 2011 by Leslie C. Allen

Published by Baker Academic
a division of Baker Publishing Group
P.O. Box 6287, Grand Rapids, MI 49516-6287
www.bakeracademic.com

Printed in the United States of America

Library of Congress Cataloging-in-Publication Data
Allen, Leslie C.
  A liturgy of grief : a pastoral commentary on Lamentations / Leslie C. Allen.
      p.   cm.
  Includes bibliographical references (p.   ) and index.
  ISBN 978-0-8010-3960-7 (pbk.)
  1. Bible. O.T. Lamentations—Commentaries. 2. Grief—Religious aspects—Christianity. 3. Pastoral care. I. Title.
BS1535.53.A45 2011
224'.307—dc23   2011016735

All translations of Lamentations are those of the author.

11   12   13   14   15   16   17   7   6   5   4   3   2   1

In keeping with biblical principles of creation stewardship, Baker Publishing Group advocates the responsible use of our natural resources. As a member of the Green Press Initiative, our company uses recycled paper when possible. The text paper of this book is composed in part of post-consumer waste.

To David, co-traveler on the journey of grief

Contents

Foreword

Strange that it did not occur to anyone earlier to do what Leslie C. Allen does in *A Liturgy of Grief.* Now that it's been done, it seems a blindingly obvious thing to do. Allen uses the Old Testament book of Lamentations to throw light on grief, and he uses contemporary examples and discussions of grief to throw light on Lamentations. The result is a much deeper insight into both. Of course others have done something of both of these. What distinguishes Allen's book is the thorough and systematic character of his discussion. He gives us a full and rich commentary on the entire book of Lamentations, illuminating both its structure and its content. And he brings to his commentary an understanding of grief that was already deeply informed both by the contemporary literature on grief, all of which he seems to have read, and by his own activities as a hospital chaplain.

Allen's commentary on Lamentations is informed not only by his acquaintance with grief and the contemporary literature on grief. It is also informed by other passages in the Old Testament; indeed, the multitude of his illuminating references to other passages of the Old Testament is nothing short of astounding. And

Allen's acquaintance with the secondary literature on Lamentations is likewise deep and wide.

This is a book to be savored. Most people will not want to read it straight through; most will find themselves unable to read it straight through. It's not complicated; it's written in simple, straightforward language. The scholarship that undergirds the discussion is presented gracefully and lucidly, and never as a display. But the book of Lamentations is itself extremely rich, deep, subtle, and moving, more than can be absorbed in one sitting. And Allen's interactive commentary is the same.

A Liturgy of Grief is at one and the same time an important contribution to our understanding of and dealing with grief, and an important contribution to our understanding of one of the supreme pieces of literature in the Old Testament. Take and savor!

Nicholas Wolterstorff

Noah Porter Professor Emeritus of
Philosophical Theology, Yale University

Senior Fellow, Institute for Advanced
Studies in Culture, University of Virginia

Preface

This book, which endeavors to integrate biblical scholarship and pastoral care, is what happens when an Old Testament professor looks at Lamentations through a chaplain's eyes. The latter perspective reflects more than eighteen hundred hours of experience as a volunteer chaplain at a local hospital. I am grateful to its spiritual care department for the opportunities I have been given and for all I have learned from colleagues and patients over the years. (In this book, patients' names have been altered and few medical details given for the sake of confidentiality.) Listening to patients' stories led me to read over a score of personal grief accounts, such as C. S. Lewis's *A Grief Observed*, and to study grief manuals, and I have correlated Lamentations with what I have learned. What emerges is that Lamentations belongs to a genre of grief literature that is recognizable by and relevant to the modern reader not only in its general message but also in many of its details. It is bifocal, engaging in grief work from the perspective of suffering and in pastoral care from the perspective of caregiving. I have been encouraged by the forays Old Testament scholars have been making into the realm of psychology to explain the book of Lamentations—Gous (1992), Joyce (1993), Reimer (2002), and Labahn (2002).

I am most grateful to my friend and colleague David Augsburger, professor of pastoral counseling, to whom the book is dedicated, for reading the manuscript and making insightful observations that have improved it. Nicholas Wolterstorff, author of *Lament for a Son*, has done me the great honor of writing the foreword. As usual, I have appreciated the staff and resources of Fuller's Hubbard Library and the painstaking work of Susan Wood of Faculty Publications Services.

I also want to thank my daughter Miriam and her partner, Sheryl, for sharing their particular expertise.

The five chapters in the book of Lamentations are really five separate poems, and they are treated as such in this commentary. The verse numbering in our Bibles represents stanzas of mostly three lines in the first and second poems, and stanzas of two lines in the fourth poem. On the other hand, the verses in the fifth poem denote individual poetic lines, while in the third poem the verse numbering refers to lines that fall into stanzas that have three lines. The numbering used in my translation follows the convention of verse numbering, except that in the third poem the stanza numbers have been added in parentheses. The notes on the translation and the Scripture index employ chapter and verse references to Lamentations.

The manuscript of this book was completed in April 2010 and submitted according to contract to Hendrickson Publishers, to whom I am grateful for the encouragement and support they gave me. However, later that year, a week before I was to receive galley proofs, they passed on their academic books to Baker Academic. I am very grateful for the way the team at Baker Academic welcomed me and for their unstinting commitment to the book.

Abbreviations

GNT	Good News Translation
KJV	King James Version
NAB	New American Bible
NEB	New English Bible
NIV	New International Version
NJB	New Jerusalem Bible
NJPS	New Jewish Publication Society Version
NRSV	New Revised Standard Version
REB	Revised English Bible
RSV	Revised Standard Version

Introduction

Tears, Talk, and Time

Raymond was brought to the hospital late one evening, as a precaution against suicide. He was a fine man in his mid-twenties, assisting the youth pastor at his church and dedicated to helping teenagers. Now he needed help. A few months before, his parents had died, one after the other, two bitter blows. Then he learned his girlfriend was dead of an overdose. It was all too much. He was brought by ambulance to this locked psychiatric unit.

The next day a request was made by the staff for a chaplain to visit. When I arrived, I gently woke Raymond out of an exhausted sleep. Bleary-eyed, he sat up in bed and said, "All I want to do is sleep." I was glad to hear him demonstrate this safe form of denial. It made me realize his stay would not be an extended one, and so this was likely to be my only visit. I also realized that this was not the occasion for a long pastoral interchange. What short message could I leave about the way forward? I thought for a moment and said, "I want to leave three words with you, Raymond: tears, talk, and time." I added a brief sentence to each word and then told him to go back to sleep and remember those three words when he woke up. "And God bless you."

Raymond's traumatic grief brings to mind the book of Lamentations, though its grief is a chorus of mourning voiced by a community of survivors. This book of five poems, in the form of five chapters, certainly responds to its calamity in terms of tears, talk, and time. It responds to deep sorrow by bringing to the surface what lies buried far down, originally beyond tears and beyond words. As we read and ponder these poems together, we will encounter many tears, for the book comes from a Mediterranean culture that was able to express its emotions freely when necessary. Tears needed to flow as an outlet for pent-up emotions, and regularly in the book grief is literally poured out as tears: *She sobs and sobs*; *Water streams from my eyes*; *I am crying my eyes out*; *Let your tears run down like a torrent day and night*; *Streams of water run down from my eyes*. No wonder Kathleen O'Connor called her commentary *Lamentations and the Tears of the World*.

There is a lesson here that those of us from stiff-upper-lip northern cultures badly need to learn. Nicholas Wolterstorff, in grieving for his son, asserted, "I shall look at the world through tears. Perhaps I shall see things that dry-eyed I could not see" (1987, 26). If tears do not come, at least one must experience a lump in the throat and periods of deep sadness. Sadness must be allowed to permeate one's life, so it can gradually do its cleansing work. There is a Yiddish proverb that calls tears the soap of the soul. The release, rather than the bottling up, of inarticulate emotion is a valuable first aid to be applied over and over again to the raw wounds of grief.

Talk is the most obvious feature of the five long poems. In the first four there is talking for and with the grieving community, while in the fifth the community at last talks back in its own prayer. All the way through the poems, the purpose of talking is to articulate grief, to face up to haunting memories with the defining clarity of speech, and to talk through emotions and reduce them to words, words that still hurt, but (one hopes) at a slightly lower level on the pain scale. Sandy Broyard, mourning her husband's lost battle with prostate cancer, describes the value of words as "pulling forwards and through" (2005, 55). In Shakespeare's *Macbeth* the bereaved Macduff is told, "Give sorrow words: the grief that does not speak / Whispers the o'er-fraught heart, and bids it break." Dorothee Soelle has written of the need "to find a language that leads out of the uncomprehended suffering that makes us mute, a language of lament, of crying, of pain" (1975, 70); she warns that silence can lead to the utter despair of suicide.

The poems keep on telling the grief story because they have to, for survival's sake. "Every time you say something, you're getting a little more of the poison out of your system by verbalizing that horrendous thought" (Barkin et al. 2004, 35). The old story is always breaking news to those who grieve. The poems instinctively know it must be told and retold. Kübler-Ross and Kessler explain this storytelling as the pain of the mind trying to catch up with the pain of the heart: "The pain is in your heart, while your mind lingers on the facts of the story, reenacting and recalling the scene of the crime against your heart" (2005, 62–63), and so helping to lessen the pain there.

Tears and talk are safety valves. Time, just as necessary, works indirectly. We conventionally speak of time as a healer. Yet a wound heals over time only with proper tending. In a similar way, time creates room for the processing of grief, and it is this processing that holds out hope of healing. It takes time for the mind to catch up with the heart. "People live on best after calamity . . . by facing it and measuring its dimensions" (Hillers 1992, 4). Every experience of grief has its own timetable; its pace must be respected, whether slower or quicker than others expect. Its duration depends on a number of individual, variable factors and is often too slow for the observer. "The dynamics of each person's sorrow must be

3

allowed to work themselves out without judgment" (Wolterstorff 1987, 56). Nevertheless, it will perhaps be disappointing to readers of the book of Lamentations to discover that closure for the grief never comes. The happy ending we all want for those who are suffering does not yet materialize in this case. The distress of the final poem is as evident as that of the first. Yet the book does reach a turning point, a resolution that is reachable from the book's own perspective. The journey of grief continues, but a milestone on that journey is attained. No wonder that one of the lessons taught in the third poem is to *wait patiently.*

Trauma: The Source of This Grief

What is the nature of the grief that pervades the book? It is a very specific and traumatic type of loss and change that has befallen a community and left it shattered. There is widespread scholarly agreement that this major disruption is to be related to the tragedy of 586 BCE. The bare bones of the tragedy are sketched in 2 Kings 25:1–12. The passage gives a dispassionate account of the historical events of 588–586 BCE in a corner of the Babylonian Empire. It briefly tells the story of the invasion of the vassal state of Judah to punish its rebellion, of the long siege of Jerusalem and its eventual fall, of the vassal king's capture, and of the systematic destruction of the city and the deportation of its citizens.

The story has been supplied with a passionate introduction in 2 Kings 24:19–20, which an awkward chapter division may make us overlook. It views the tragedy from a theological perspective that emotionally interprets the history in terms of the vassal king's previously *doing evil in the sight of the* LORD, *just as Jehoiakim* [his predecessor] *had done* and of *the* LORD's *anger,* so intense that *he thrust them from his presence.* The book of Lamentations has a similar blend of history, theology, and emotion. But, whereas 2 Kings presents these elements to the reader separately on the dinner plate, as it were, here they are mixed together in a salad bowl. The mix lends religious vehemence to the grief of survivors left in Judah to which Lamentations bears witness. Divine anger and rejection in response to human provocation are taken seriously as providential keys to the disaster. Emotion pervades not only the book's theology but also its reliving of historical details. For instance, we readers will be told more about the mass starvation of 2 Kings 25:3 than we ever wanted to know.

Tradition: Ancient Idioms of Grieving

Though its form varies greatly, grief is a universal, cross-cultural reaction to loss and change, as anthropological studies summarized by Archer (1999, 52–54) have shown. How could so tragic a grief as that caused by the calamity in 586 BCE be processed? There were national traditions, reflected in the book of Lamentations, on which the survivors could draw. The same can hardly be said of the culture in which most of us readers now live; contemporary Western culture provides little space for grief. Sixty years ago, after my mother died, I recall the drapes kept firmly closed at the front windows in the daytime, my older brothers wearing black armbands on their coats, and a black tie replacing my school tie for a long time. Now a funeral service may be reduced to an ostensibly more healthy form of a celebration of life. In general, church services can be uncomfortable and unsatisfying for the one who grieves, for these services may reflect an aversion to sorrow that takes no account of the somber realities of life. All this cultural aversion handicaps the necessary task of grieving because one is ill prepared. Everyone has a right to grieve and an obligation to respect the grief of others.

Older cultures gave grief much more respect, regarding it as a necessary part of lives that were potentially fragile at every level. Like other cultures, Israelite culture had its traditions of grieving. Apart from nonverbal mourning rituals, there were grooves, as it were, within the social framework of oral communication along which the expression of grief could move with a measure of ease. It is important for readers to recognize these culturally normal channels through which the text flows in order to articulate grief.

The first of the traditional speech forms is the funeral dirge, in reaction to bereavement. There is a fine, extended example in 2 Samuel 1, where David mourns the deaths of Saul, his king, and Jonathan, his friend. The dirge typically employed, and often began with, a shriek, *ekh* or *ekhah* in Hebrew, which introduced an exclamatory statement of loss. In the book of Lamentations the longer form marks the beginning of the first, second, and fourth poems. I have translated it *How terrible that . . . !*

The dirge was capable of adaptation to other situations of grief besides bereavement, and in Lamentations its conventions are used to mourn the general calamity of the siege and fall of Jerusalem and its ramifications. In the dirge, the descriptions focus on contrasting a sunny past with the dark storm that has now blotted out life's sunshine. Such contrasts appear frequently in the book and permit the articulation of what the tragedy meant in detailed respects that were important to those who yearned for what they had lost.

The dirge told the grief story, as for example in Jeremiah 9:21 (or 21–22 according to such versions as the NAB, NJB, and GNT). Despite the religious flavor that Lamentations has in other aspects, the book makes good use of the essentially secular nature of the dirge, which characteristically did not mention God. So Lamentations can take human suffering seriously (Moore 1983) and allow the multifaceted aspects of the human side of grief to be fully explored. When lives are shattered by change, their range of human interactions is fragmented. The dirge gave permission for broken piece after broken piece to be picked up and wept over. The book draws heavily on the dirge tradition and finds it an invaluable aid in the expression of grief.

Another tradition that dealt with grief and was available to use was the lament psalm. There are sixty-five of these in the book of

Psalms, nearly half of the total collection, a proportion that testifies to their perceived need and value in the precarious living of ancient times. The lament psalm comes in two forms, communal and individual, and is essentially a prayer to God, unlike the dirge. Like the dirge, it makes room for a grieving description of a crisis, but now as part of a plea to Yahweh to intervene positively and put right what is woefully wrong. Readers will discover that in the first two poems there is a creative movement from dirge to lament (Linafelt 2000, 43) and so implicitly from a necessary bemoaning of what is past to looking to a future that God can help these sufferers to achieve eventually. The fifth poem consists of such a lament, one of which also opens and closes the third poem. Both the dirge and the lament psalm provide necessary perspectives for the outworking of grief in the book.

The lament psalm has often been called a complaint in scholarly circles. However, Craig Broyles (1989) has made an excellent case for identifying a subtype of lament psalm, again both communal and individual, that in twenty-one psalms represents a shriller, more strident prayer that may appropriately monopolize the name "complaint" in the sense of complaining to God about what God has or has not done. If one reads the examples of complaint in the Psalms, it is not difficult to recognize its presence in the closing six lines of the fifth poem in Lamentations. This is an important phenomenon since the climax of the book is involved. In the exposition, I will carefully point out parallel texts from the Psalms and let their meaning guide the exegesis of this key passage.

A further tradition that has been claimed to explain Lamentations is the so-called city lament, which was a feature of much older Mesopotamian culture and literature. Typically, a city lament mourned the gods' destruction of a city (Lee 2002, 38–39); its affinities with the representations of Zion in Lamentations probably result from the expression of a common experience within a similar religious culture (Ferris 1992, 167–75; Lee 2002, 37–39; Berlin).

The distinctive role of Zion in the book not only as the representative of the congregation but also as a model for them to follow recalls the Israelite tradition of professional women mourners who took the lead on behalf of the bereaved, encouraging them to break into tears (2 Chron. 35:25; Jer. 9:17–18, 20), and suggests the participation of one of their number. If so, the function of such a female singer is here strikingly developed from mourning to engaging in prayers of lament.

A Liturgy of Grief

The book of Lamentations is best understood as the script of a liturgy intended as a therapeutic ritual. It was composed for the survivors of the calamity of 586 BCE who were left behind in Judah, and the liturgy was performed at the site of the ruined temple to mourn their losses. Zechariah 7:5 is relevant, for it refers to the early postexilic period as a time of continuing fasting and mourning that had been carried out annually in the fifth and seventh months "for the past seventy years." (The fifth month was when the temple was destroyed; see 2 Kings 25:8–9.) Within Lamentations, it is significant that in two places direct address to God in prayer is associated with the temple. The first is in Lamentations 1:10, where mention of foreigners aggressively entering the temple is followed by an abrupt turning to God in second-person address. The second is in Lamentations 5:18, which introduces the closing section of ardent prayer with a reference to the devastated temple area. As one might expect from a poetic grief account, the text is allusive in its historical references. However, analysis of the language used in the poems has shown that its transitional character fits the exilic period, from 586 to 520 BCE (Dobbs-Allsopp 1998).

The coherence of the book is apparent when it is regarded in terms of a story. The verbalization of grief essentially consists of the telling of a complex story, in a piecemeal fashion but eventually covering the basic facts of loss and change. In this case the poems follow a loose pattern of consecutive narrative. Most of the grieving consists of intrusive memories that vividly recall episodes of the long siege. Such flashbacks are typical of grief: "Even though I am here, I know that the smallest thing—a song, a sound, a smell—can send me back there" (Hood 2008, 156). This looking backward to the siege is especially true of the first two poems. The fourth poem gradually shifts to the closing days of the siege and the frustrated efforts of priests and others, including the king, to find refuge after the city fell. The fifth poem focuses on the postwar occupation of Jerusalem and Judah. So the poems follow a story line, incorporating a collection of assorted but roughly consecutive narratives.

Another aspect of the development of a story is that it works toward resolution of an earlier complication. This happens in the book of Lamentations, although readers are in danger of regarding the book as unfinished because they look in vain for the closure to grief they would like to see, in the form of acceptance or accommodation and moving on with a renewed quality of life despite unforgettable loss. In personal terms, acceptance "does not mean forgetting the person we have lost, but instead placing that relationship somewhere inside us where it's comfortable so we can carry on with our lives" (Bouvard and Gnadu 1998, 33). But there is no acceptance here. Rather, the fifth poem presents the congregation's prayer of lament. This prayer represents the attainment of a sustained effort made in the first three poems to encourage such a prayer as an aid in coming to terms with grief. The effort is most obvious in the explicit call to prayer in Lamentations 3:40–41, *Let us lift our hearts . . . to God in heaven*, and the supplying of a model prayer in the next lines. But model prayers have not been lacking in the first two poems (1:11–16, 18–22; 2:20–22). They have been placed on the lips of a character called Zion, who represents the listening congregation and has the roles of their "model and teacher" (Berges 2000, 10). From the perspective of the fifth poem, she prays in order to encourage the community to bring their own prayer, suggesting in her prayers the lines their prayer should follow.

Moreover, the third poem begins and ends with examples of individual prayers of lament taken from the speaker's experience, which like Zion's prayers are meant to stimulate the congregation to break into their own articulation of grief, when they are ready. The poems work toward an intended goal. That goal is congregational prayer, which represents not the closure of grief but a turning point in the communal grieving that bravely and even defiantly challenges their suffering and expresses a longing to move beyond it.

The book's coherence relates to its present form as a completed liturgy for a memorial service. This is not to deny that it may have grown by stages and so reflects a compositional unity. For instance, a feature of the first four poems that is invisible to the reader of the English text is that they are self-contained. Each poem is written as a separate alphabetic acrostic that uses in turn each letter of the Hebrew alphabet at the beginning of stanzas in the first, second, and fourth poems and at the beginning of each line of the stanzas in the third poem. Ronald Knox's version (1956) does represent the alphabetic sequencing, for instance, "Alone she dwells . . . / Be sure she weeps . . . / Cruel the suffering . . ." and so on in the first poem, but it has to resort to contrived translation. There is a peculiarity about the order of the Hebrew letters. While the first poem follows the usual order, the next three reverse the order of two letters that correspond to "o" and "p" in the English alphabet. This order is attested elsewhere, but the difference is striking. The first poem may represent an initial attempt that was later supplemented with the other poems for the liturgy. Hunter (1996) has argued that the first half of the first poem represents a core that the rest of the book expands. Does this function reflect a poem written subsequently to introduce an extant collection? Its generality and comprehensiveness may point to that conclusion.

As the book stands, there is a growing intensity in the first three poems. In the exposition I compare this trend with the development in the first two chapters of the book of Joel, as far as Joel 2:17. Both texts move steadily and with increasing passion toward a dynamic appeal to the congregation to utter a prayer of repentance, and they both support that appeal with an assurance of Yahweh's grace and compassion. The third poem represents an interim climax, to which the factor of the intensified acrostic, mentioned earlier, draws attention. The real climax of the book is to come in the communal prayer of the fifth poem. The third poem, by issuing its summons to the congregation to pray, points forward to their response in the final poem. The theology in the middle of the third poem, with its providential sweep beyond judgment to salvation, is the handmaid of pastoral care.

In the liturgy, I hear three voices speaking. The third voice is the communal one in the last poem. The second voice is that of a woman personifying Zion. Gottwald has called Zion "an imaginative figure who both embodies and stands apart from particular Judahites" (1993, 167). She functions as a role model for the congregation meeting in the city and is meant to inspire their own reaction in due course. This modeling is evident from a comparison of Lamentations 2:16 with 3:46. Zion is addressed with the words, *Staring openmouthed at you were all your enemies*, while the congregation is encouraged to say of itself, *Staring openmouthed at us are all our enemies*. Zion is a representation of the congregation projected onto a screen, as it were, where in an ideal way she voices its suffering and expresses its grief. She is the poster girl for the responses to tragedy the community should make.

And whose is the first voice? I suggest that a pastoral mentor is speaking; he plays a number of roles in the first four poems. Himself a member of the suffering community, he endeavors to guide them through their distress and engage in grief work on their behalf. Occasionally in communal laments in the book of Psalms, the worship leader speaks for a while as an individual, expressing a conviction the rest of the congregation is not yet ready to aspire to and so guiding them toward a stronger faith (Pss. 44:4–6; 74:12–17; 123:1). In this case the liturgy leader assumes a much larger role of a similar kind. He mentors members of the community by giving expression to the grief he and they have in common, turning incoherent feelings into words and explaining the experiences they have all been through. He acts as a reporter in the first two poems, surveying and describing different aspects of their cataclysmic loss. He is also an interpreter of their loss, claiming that the congregation should take responsibility for what had happened and yet affirming their sense of grievance (see the section "Trajectories of Grief, Guilt, and Grievance" below).

In the third poem this worship leader, mentor, and reporter presents himself as a wounded healer, another role model for the congregation alongside Zion. He gives a personal testimony of surviving merited suffering on an earlier occasion and then preaches a sermon that draws on divine resources for resilience and recovery, before appealing to the congregation to pray a prayer of repentance and giving another testimony that respects their grievances. He can speak with true sympathy, a reaction of fellow feeling that emanates from a significant overlap of suffering experienced previously in his own life.

In the fourth poem he leaves time for the community to react to his counseling by resuming a reporter's role and describing its suffering further, but at the close he echoes the hope of the third poem.

Then at last, in the fifth poem, the third voice speaks. The congregation, duly taught by its mentor and nurtured by the role modeling that he and Zion have provided, is ready to articulate its grief in its own prayer. Grief continues, but the congregation has reached a turning point and starts to move forward in turning to God.

Thus the poems make up a therapeutic ritual to deal with grief (see Rando 1993, 313–31; Sanders 1999, 252–57). It is a ritual of transition that sensitively takes the congregation through the emotional and spiritual trauma of their losses, helps them toward a new start, and finally involves them in a creative response of their own that they are ready to make in the final poem.

Commentators often remark that there is no fourth voice—the voice of God—that takes part in the liturgy. This absence accords with the admission in Lamentations 2:9, *Her prophets found no revelation from Yahweh*, and with the broader prophetic tradition that links divine silence with disobedience on the part of God's people. In more general terms, it agrees with the phenomenon that the most spiritual of grievers encounter a silent, distant God. However, in two respects, though the voice of God is not directly heard, it is overheard. First, the preacher imparts hope by testifying to having heard God's reassuring voice in another time of grief: *you said, "Don't be afraid"* (3:57). Second, notice should be taken of the way the book freely mentions the *mouth* of God (1:18; 3:38) as having engaged in past speech and God's having *ordered* or *given orders* (1:10, 17; 2:17; 3:37) and *announced* a day of judgment (1:21). This second phenomenon may imply that the reading of religious texts accompanied the liturgy and that these repeated references to divine speech allude to them.

Albrektson (1963, 233–36) has urged that there are quotations of Deuteronomy 28 in Lamentations. His most feasible examples are Deuteronomy 28:41 in Lamentations 1:5 and 18; Deuteronomy 28:44 in Lamentations 1:5 again; Deuteronomy 28:53 in Lamentations 2:20; and Deuteronomy 28:65 in Lamentations 1:3. Although he admits that verses 47–68 are generally regarded as later additions to the text, he himself is doubtful whether such editing occurred. Berlin recognizes the cases in the first poem—except for the one in 1:18—as echoes of Deuteronomy 28 but does not mention the problem. Brandscheidt (1983, 210–14) simply accepts the cases in the first poem as already showing familiarity with the later growth. This seems to be a wise conclusion, even if it means placing the book later during the exile.

Within the poems, there seems to be awareness of other texts. The theological importance of Zion is illustrated by references to specific psalms (Pss. 48:2; 50:2 in Lam. 2:15; Ps. 76:12 in Lam. 4:12), while Lamentations 5:18–19 echoes an aspect of the Zion tradition (Albrektson 1963, 224–28). A common feature of the book is allusion to authoritative traditions known to us from the preexilic prophetic books. According to Lamentations 1:17; 2:17; and 3:37, what was evidently a prophetic program was *ordered* by Yahweh. It is difficult to pin down particular quotations, apart from *my poor people's catastrophe* (Lam. 2:11; 3:48; 4:10 from Jer. 8:21); the plural use of a typical phrase from Jeremiah, "terror from everywhere around" (in Lam. 2:22); in Lamentations 4:17 verbal echoes of Isaiah 30:7; and in Lamentations 5:21 a quotation from what we know as Jeremiah 31:18.

However, the blatant description of the tragedy in terms of hostile divine intervention and dire human consequences (Lam. 1:12–15; 2:1–9), a pairing that is copied in the testimony that opens the third poem, seems in general to reflect the program set out by the prophets. It is evidently based on the announcement of disaster that is so widespread in the prophetic literature, where this standard pattern is followed. In turn, the book's insistence on Zion's or Judah's sinfulness sounds like an echo of the accusation that regularly precedes the announcement in prophetic oracles of disaster, although appeal is also made to the overall prophetic program as a source of hope (3:38). The prophetic literature included the promise of *good fortune* as well as pronouncements of *misfortunes*. Beyond all expectation Israel was to rise like a phoenix from its ashes. In the third poem we will also find awareness of a fund of positive theological truths that are found throughout the Old Testament. So God's voice is overheard from afar at crucial places in the book, both as having heralded in the past the community's time of suffering and as offering newness of life for a future beyond that suffering.

Trajectories of Grief, Guilt, and Grievance

Grief comes in many shapes, shades, and sizes. The grief of Lamentations is of a traumatic, collective, and complicated nature, which counselors and pastoral caregivers distinguish from "normal" grief and which displays exaggerated and prolonged features. *Grief* is a general term used of the whole process of adjusting to loss and change. It is also used of a particular part of the process, a reaction of distress. In the latter sense, grief, guilt, and grievance represent three trajectories that run through Lamentations. I can recall only two cases of such a mix told to me by patients, cases quite different from each other. The differences are a warning that the exposition will need to study carefully the relationship between the three trajectories.

Sarah, an older woman, had been a foster mother for many years. A short time before I visited her, she had slapped a naughty child, who reported her to the social worker. Her fostering license was taken away, and now her life was empty—in fact, when she died the next week of complications following her surgery, the death certificate might have specified a broken heart as a contributing factor. She realized she had done wrong but protested to me that her punishment had been excessive in view of her many, unblemished years of service. I had been a foster parent at an earlier period of my life, and so I was deeply moved as Sarah told me of her grief in which guilt and grievance were tangled.

In the other case, Tom, a chronically disabled patient, could hardly wait to tell me that his parents would have nothing to do with him and that his only sister would not answer his phone calls. He was in great distress. "Do you have any visitors?" I asked. "My wife drives in most evenings," he replied. "She's Mexican," he added in a noticeably apologetic tone. I wondered whether that had anything to do with his family rejecting him, but I did not ask. I did know the couple lived a long way from the hospital. I felt I ought to gently suggest that the next time his wife visited him, he should tell her he loved her and how grateful he was that she was family. Tom thought and nodded. His grief and sense of grievance had a measure of guilt attached.

There is an impressive consensus among commentators, such as Hillers, Re'emi, Westermann, and O'Connor, that the theme of Lamentations is the articulation of grief, but apart from O'Connor, who wrote from the depths of her own grief, they are not sensitive to its presence. Gottwald has characterized the book as a "project of 'grief work' by which [those who grieved] bridged the gap between primal grief and outrage at the fall of Jerusalem and the ethics and theology by means of which their people interpreted public events and oriented their lives" (1993, 173). The pervasive use of alphabetic acrostics in the Hebrew is commonly interpreted as indicating the totality of grief, all-encompassing from A to Z. This also seems to be the acrostic's role in the course of a lament psalm, Psalm 25, while in the hymns of Psalms 111 and 145 it signifies a totality of praiseworthiness, and in the tribute of Proverbs 31:10–31 it conveys an impression of the complete wife. The suggestion has also been made that in Lamentations the acrostic aims to reinstate stability and order, but the dominance of grief in the book favors the notion that its main role is to reinforce it.

In these pages, grief is intertwined with loss and change as an inevitable reaction. A keyword runs through the original Hebrew whose overall usage registers this instinctive combination. It occurs six times, and I have translated it *devastated*. The translation is a useful one because, like the Hebrew word, it can cover the objective facts of suffering and/or the subjective feelings they evoke. The term occurs at the close of the book, in Lamentations 5:18, to describe the ruined temple site: *Mount Zion . . . lies devastated.* At the opening of the book, in 1:4, it has as its subject the broken city gates through which pilgrims no longer passed. It is used in a metaphorical way that blends objective and subjective aspects: Zion's gates *feel devastated.* Loss and grief are so bonded that grief is perceived as permeating the material evidence of the loss. In 1:13 Zion exclaims that the tragedy, viewed as divine punishment, *left me feeling devastated*. She goes on in 1:16 to subtly allude to the resentful distress of the listening congregation: *My children feel devastated that the enemy has prevailed*. In 3:11 the mentor's testimony about his own suffering echoes Zion's cry in 1:13 by saying that Yahweh's punishment *left me devastated*. In 4:5 the term is used of the effect of the long siege on one group of its victims, formerly rich people, who now *lay devastated in the streets*. Here again objective and subjective factors are combined. Apart from this keyword, grief manifests itself constantly through the book in the combination of a telling of objective facts of suffering and a reaction of subjective feelings of distress.

A second trajectory for the book takes the form of guilt. "Guilt reactions . . . are a normal and expectable aspect of the grief experience" (Rando 1984, 31), whether legitimate or not. Here they are claimed to be legitimate and appropriate to the situation. The distinctive presence of guilt endorses the message that is sounded loud and clear in the canonical preexilic prophets, that Judah's downfall, when it came, was to be no mere consequence of political rebellion against a secular power but a theological event by which divine intervention would punish Judah's spiritual rebellion. The vehement language of Yahweh's active hostility against Zion in 1:12–15 and 2:1–9 has been misunderstood by some commentators in terms of angry protest directed at God. Its true nature can be gathered from the fact that the recapitulation of this hostility in 3:43–47 is prefaced with a call for repentance and confession of sinning in lines 40–42.

Hunter (1996, 115, 145–46), appealing to Lamentations 1:5, 11, has fittingly looked behind agency to causality, behind Yahweh's responsive role as executor, using Babylon as an instrument, to Israel's initiatory role as the real cause underlying the divine intervention. The tragedy of 586 BCE was to be acknowledged as God's punitive intervention, the mentor urges in 2:1–9. No wonder his teaching assistant, Zion, anticipates him in 1:12–15 and is made to exclaim in 1:18, *Yahweh is the one in the right, because I defied (the words of) his mouth.* Two supporting stratagems are used in the book to teach the same lesson. First, divine anger comes to the fore in the second poem and is echoed in the mentor's first testimony in the third. It is to be understood as the awesome reaction to human sinfulness. Second, mention of human guilt and/or Yahweh's intervention that presupposes it occurs at significant junctures in the fourth and fifth poems.

In the Christian canon the book of Lamentations has been placed among the Prophets, next to the book of Jeremiah. However, in the older Hebrew canon of Scripture it belongs to another section, the Writings. The repositioning was due to an early tradition that Jeremiah wrote it, miscuing from 2 Chronicles 35:25. The tradition was already known to the Greek version, which was probably produced around 50 BCE. This tradition, which attempts to break through the anonymity of the book, has been revived by Lee (2002) in the case of the first voice in Lamentations 1 and 2 and in 3:46–51 and 4:1–16, 21–22 on the grounds of linguistic parallels with the book of Jeremiah. I have found this tradition of little value in expounding the five poems. Nevertheless, the placement is helpful in that it puts Lamentations at the heart of the prophetic literature, whose fundamental message the book avidly endeavored to teach.

For many people, guilt is not a major factor in the processing of their grief. However, there are situations in which it looms large, for example when a drunk driver has caused downright harm. In fact, Alcoholics Anonymous (AA) is a modern counterpart to Lamentations in its insistence on guilt. Not that the organization uses the term, because it has good reason not to. For an alcoholic, the word is a dangerous one, heard not as "guilt" but as "shame," an emotion that can encourage defeatist, purely mental self-recrimination liable to drive him or her back to drinking. Instead, not at an initial stage but at subsequent steps in the twelve-step program, the movement teaches and implements processes of confession to God and another human being, of commitment to God's help, and of a pragmatic making of amends for specific wrongdoing, where possible. The necessity of taking responsibility for harm done, as an important means of regaining a clean and sober life, lies at the heart of the program.

The mentor of the community in the book of Lamentations has a kindred spirit in the AA sponsor who nurses along a particular recovering alcoholic and is committed to the progress of his or her charge. The handling of grief-stricken guilt is a task known both to the ancient mentor and to the contemporary sponsor. However, although there is overlap, the demand for accountability that Lamentations makes is not the same. It does not go so far as the human righting of wrongs the community has done. Instead, it is concerned with an intermediate goal, an admission that the punishment of sins was necessary and just, and it looks to God to right the wrongs done to the community. So guilt, in a legal sense, is a reasonable description of what was required, though theologically it transcends a purely forensic significance. The mentor sought a guilty plea to accompany grief so that the admission might trigger God's forgiveness of their sins and the fresh start predicted in the prophetic books—that "hope" for which Paul continued to look (Acts 26:6–7; 28:20). The attribution of guilt has a larger role in the liturgy as a whole. It is the start of a persuasive process of finding meaning for tragedy, a process that will culminate positively in the third poem, with its message that in God's overall purposes *good fortune* can be the intended sequel of such *misfortunes* (line 38). The confession of guilt has grace as its goal.

The third trajectory in the book is grievance, a theme that is liable to make readers uncomfortable. Does not grievance conflict with admitted guilt? And it hardly seems to be an acceptable spiritual response to suffering. Yet from a psychological perspective such anger is "a basic emotional response to loss" (Archer 1999, 70) and so a normal part of the process of grief. It is not surprising therefore that it is assigned significant space in the first two poems. The stage theory of grief lists anger as one of its five regular manifestations, after numb disbelief and yearning for the loss, and before depression (or at least profound and pervasive sadness) and acceptance; moreover, grief resulting from traumatic events—such as the book of Lamentations reflects—has been found to generate a higher degree of anger (Maciejewski et al. 2007, 712, 722). Looked at in this light, the book comes across as a comprehensive mingling of the three middle components—nostalgic yearning, deep sadness, and angry protest—with another item thrown into the mix, a sense of guilt. Advocates of the stage theory do not insist on strict sequencing, while there is a widely held view that the process of grief consists of a jumble of responses, disordered emotional debris. The book appears to reflect this view. The congregation's silence until the fifth poem implicitly signifies the prolonging of shocked numbness, which, as characteristically in cases of traumatic loss, hampered the expression of their own grief and necessitated the pastoral efforts of the first four poems. Those efforts eventually enabled the people to break out of the spiritual inertia in which they were sunk.

Anger, then, has a part to play in the outworking of grief. "Despite impressive evidence that unacknowledged anger causes psychological, behavioral, social, and physical problems, anger is a poorly tolerated and often misunderstood emotion in Western societies" (Rando 1993, 464). Israel's culture was realistic in finding room for expressions of grievance in the Psalms and the prophetic books. An instructive example of the latter occurs in Isaiah 10:5–19, which announces that Yahweh's punishment of Israel was to be followed by the punishment of Yahweh's human instrument, Assyria, for going beyond divinely set limits. This prophetic message is clearly a response to a sense of grievance at what was regarded as excessive suffering, for which the human enemy was blamed rather than God. It is this sort of grievance, as an element in a complex situation, that pervades the book of Lamentations. Judah had been the victim as well as the culprit, the injured party as well as the guilty party, sinned against as well as sinning.

At this point it is helpful to compare contemporary grief in response to a traumatic experience because it makes such grievance easier to understand. Abigail Carter (2008) calls one section of her tale of personal loss from 9/11 "the cleansing winds of anger." Certainly the grief of homicide survivors includes intense anger. When a close relative is randomly killed by a drunk or speeding driver or is murdered, no one is surprised at the family's angry desire for the offender to be caught and for justice to be manifestly done (Lord 1990, 19–22). It is in this spirit that the grievances of Lamentations are to be viewed. The mentor counsels that his people's deep anger over their wartime and postwar experiences should be brought to Yahweh as the one who has the providential power to bring about justice.

Accordingly, in the first poem, Zion, the congregation's role model, is heard praying about their enemies' acts of injustice and bringing them to God to resolve (1:21–22). The third poem provides an assurance that God takes notice of unjust behavior perpetrated during the postwar occupation (3:34–36). Moreover, in that poem the mentor cites as an example in his second testimony his prayer for justice over his own undeserved suffering at the hands of his enemies (3:52–66). The fourth poem closes with the mentor's assurance that Edom, Judah's archenemy, will get the comeuppance it deserves. The prayer in the fifth poem brings to the divine notice outrages committed by the occupying forces—and in the closing lines dares to express a measure of anger against God. The trajectory of grievance, like the trajectories of grief and guilt, runs through the book as evidence of raw and impassioned sorrow that cries out for relief. The hand stretched out in appeals for compassion and help turns at times into a clenched fist, and this is right and acceptable in the outworking of deep anguish, especially in its early stages.

The Fifth Poem as Finale

The last poem, the shortest of the five, is the real articulation of grief on the community's part, to which the earlier poems have been a preamble. Primed by what it has been taught, the congregation now poignantly speaks with its own voice. Of course, all that the two other voices, those of the mentor and of Zion, have said has doubtless brought relief, since the mentor is one of their own, having suffered what they have suffered and more besides, while Zion is a dramatic version of themselves. Yet without this particular articulation in the fifth poem, something would have been seriously lacking. "The sufferer himself must find a way to express and identify his suffering; it is not sufficient to hear someone else speak on his behalf" (Soelle 1975, 76). So their speaking out is necessary; it spells substantial progress in the processing of their grief. In fact, taking a stand of their own marks a turning point within grief, for which the mentor and Zion have been working so diligently and waiting so long. The congregation's speaking spells a change for the better and a decisive step toward coming to terms with the tragedy that has befallen them.

So much has been learned to give them an insight into their suffering. The three trajectories, the gut-felt themes of grief, guilt, and grievance, all come to a head in the fifth poem. Here the guilt, brief though the references to it are, is thoughtfully explored and set at structurally salient places in tones of sincere apology. Grief is covered in both its subjective and objective aspects, the latter now relating to the postwar occupation. The congregation has appreciated the flashbacks of the earlier poems, the necessary emotional reliving of horrible memories and the speaking of the unspeakable.

Now they can move to contemporary causes of distress. The grief is permeated with resentful grievance over their enemies' ill treatment, from which they have all been suffering in a multitude of ways. The community makes the three trajectories its own and creatively develops them as it echoes them.

The fifth poem is a prayer. That is not the most natural place for the grief-stricken to find themselves at, nor is it where the book itself began. It began with a voicing of the dirge, a step beyond a shocked and mute preoccupation with tragedy, but still a step that is able only to explore the human areas to which the tragedy pertains. In the first two poems the mentor recommends going further and turning to God in prayer, and the listening congregation hears Zion comply. The underlying reason for praying is bound up with the special nature of the catastrophe as divine punishment. The God who had torn down was the only one to turn to for restoration (Hunter 1996, 146). In the fifth poem the congregation engages in its own prayer, leaning on the tradition of the lament psalms. Something of the dirge survives: the account of suffering is much longer than what one finds in a lament psalm. Their traumatic grief still needs the emotional space the dirge provides.

From the perspective of prayer, the three trajectories take on new meaning, both here and earlier in the book in prayer contexts. Grief appeals to the compassion of God, and guilt produces confession that appeals to God for forgiveness, while grievance appeals to the justice of God. In this case the close of the prayer enterprisingly draws on another prayer tradition, one not used in the book hitherto, the tradition of a complaint psalm that challenges God. It dares to remind God to keep promises earlier made to the community of faith. The resources of prayer are ransacked because the congregation knows that whatever it can do by itself is not enough. They depend on God's taking the initiative: *Restore us to yourself, so that we can be restored.*

23

Balm for the Grief-Stricken

Brevard Childs summed up the canonical value of Lamentations by saying it "serves every successive generation of the suffering faithful for whom history has become unbearable" (1979, 596). This biblical book validates grief. It is God's gift to those who grieve. Historically, Lamentations is an effort to come to terms with 586 BCE, to face up to the shock it generated, in the hope of moving beyond it. The presence of Lamentations in the Bible emanates from the subsequent endorsement of the faith community, who recognized that this liturgical text was of supreme spiritual worth and in a special way was in tune with God's own heart. The book's canonicity is striking because so much of it is concerned with human suffering and with distress over human losses. Those who grieve will resonate with the book, hearing in it echoes of their own stories and emotions.

However, I recall a patient who, having undergone a mastectomy, found it difficult to grieve because of her Christian faith. She felt she was letting God down by failing to accept what she perceived as the loss of her womanhood. She thought grief was a sign of spiritual weakness and lack of trust. It had to be stifled as dishonoring to God. Her grief, repressed, was not lessened; her fear of owning and expressing it blocked any processing. Lamentations belies such a stoic view. It pushes human suffering to the fore as an indispensable concern. As a religious liturgy, the text brought human grief right into the temple courts (see the section "A Liturgy of Grief" above).

Judaism has two titles for the book. The first is its initial word, the shocked scream *ekhah*, which I have translated *How terrible that . . . !* It comes from the dirge, a secular manifestation of grief. The second title, found in the Talmud, is *Qinoth*, which comes from the same background. It means "dirges," elegies that bemoan human loss with no reference to God. This meaning underlies the English title, Lamentations. Each of the Hebrew titles recognizes that the intent of the book is to honor human grief; the titles invest grief with spiritual value. The book sanctifies the human process of dealing with the consequences of suffering as invaluable to its victims and so to a compassionate God.

Every grief is special. The story a grieving person has to tell is both like and unlike any other. This is particularly true of the book of Lamentations, whose historical and collective nature and cultural interpretation make it so distinctive. Little attempt has been made in the exposition to draw parallels with modern experiences of communal disasters, experiences that Zinner and Williams's collection of studies (1999) analyzes. As those studies show, there is considerable overlap with grief and adaptation to change on the personal level. The communal nature of the disaster depicted in Lamentations is a significant indication of the special nature of its grief. Still, any who grieve will welcome insights from the book, despite its idiosyncrasies that they do not share. Grief creates a canon within the biblical canon, headed by the books of Job and Lamentations and the lament psalms in the book of Psalms. They all offer literary companionship. Grieving people develop a knack of welcoming what they recognize as relevant to them and ignoring the rest. No matter that these biblical resources have different approaches to suffering. No matter that Job and Lamentations stand at opposite ends of a grief spectrum that ranges from innocence to guilt. The main thing is that they all embrace grief. So they enable those who grieve to feel at home with their generalities, whereas the world around and even their Christian circle may strike them as alien and unfeeling. Here are Scriptures that stand where the grieving stand. Such literature turns grief into a spiritual pilgrimage, excruciatingly arduous though it is, and permits faith to somehow survive despite the strains put on it.

A Book for Caregivers

I use the word *caregivers* to refer primarily to the pastor, counselor, or chaplain. For these caregivers, my exposition of Lamentations offers role models for dealing compassionately with those who grieve; stories about patients may prove especially useful for counselors or chaplains as they work with clients or patients. Pastors may apply the insights to their work with individuals in their congregations or, in a communal setting, use the material in this book as the basis for a sermon series about grief and caregiving.

In addition, a friend, relative, or good Samaritan may be a caregiver. These persons may hear echoed the desperate cry at two places in the book, "Will somebody out there—anybody—please listen?" (Lam. 1:12, 18); and those who grieve are liable to buttonhole strangers. For these caregivers, the text's insights about a sympathetic listener, along with the material about the grieving process, may prove valuable.

The book of Lamentations is a tribute to caregivers in view of the dominant part played by a speaker I call the mentor (see the section "A Liturgy of Grief" above). It is the mentor who helps the community to come to terms with its calamity. Himself one of its suffering members, remarkably he is able to step forward and minister to the needs of those whom he compassionately calls "my poor people."

Sometimes all that is required of caregivers is companionable silence, especially in the early stages of grief. That was what Job's three friends supplied at first (Job 2:13). Even Jesus asked his disciples to be such caregivers in the garden of Gethsemane, as in anticipatory grief he underwent the ordeal of waiting for the worst to happen: "My soul is overwhelmed with sorrow to the point of death. Stay here and keep watch with me" (Matt. 26:38). In Lamentations the mentor needs to do more, to "weep with those who weep" (Rom. 12:15 NRSV), openly participating in their emotional turmoil. This is easier said than done. As Ella Wheeler Wilcox wrote in her poem "Solitude," "Laugh and the world laughs with you. / Weep and you weep alone" (1958, 72). But supremely the mentor gives his community words and ways to grieve by articulating their grief and directing them to helpful traditions of expressing sorrow in a coherent manner. As a fellow sufferer, he is well positioned to experience and express the community's feelings.

In the third poem, this speaker puts on the mantle of the wounded healer, sharing his own stories to help the congregation get through theirs. Like Paul, he shows Yahweh to be "the Father of compassion and the God of all comfort, who comforts us in all our troubles, so that we can comfort those in any trouble with the comfort we ourselves have received from God" (2 Cor. 1:3–4). The mentor both reveals God to be compassionate and by his mentoring shows his own compassion, which is the foremost spiritual virtue according to Colossians 3:12. He is able to call the congregation to renewed faith and hope—and yet to fall back into fresh articulation of grief in the fourth poem, as he waits for them to catch up with him.

Readers of Lamentations have the opportunity to exercise their own skills in empathy, in direct response to Zion's appeal, *Listen, peoples everywhere, and look at my anguish!* (Lam. 1:18). Empathy is the capacity to gain a sensitive understanding of another's pain that has not first been one's own. "To read literature without an empathic view gives rise to interpretations of the work that fail to appreciate the inner mental life that the author, wittingly or unwittingly, is attempting to portray" (Muslin 1984, 303). Readers' success in this task depends on immersion in the total text rather than in selected parts. The book of Lamentations, read as a whole, takes readers into the hearts and minds of grieving folk and provides an exercise in empathic listening. It sets before us a case study that challenges us to identify with the feelings expressed in the text, step by step, and to understand its cultural traditions and theological presuppositions. It also invites us to appreciate the case study within the case study, how the mentor not only takes the congregation's grief seriously but also endeavors to help them move forward in their grief and gradually align that grief with appropriate faith and hope.

What will emerge is the singularity of the grief. The chaplain walks into the patient's room as well versed as possible in his or her history and still acutely aware of a need to pick up cues from the patient and learn the other person's perspective. There is a particularity about grief that must be acknowledged and respected. This is certainly true of the grief in Lamentations. As one reads these five poems, a story emerges that is familiar only to those who have read 2 Kings and the prophetic books. There is no obvious New Testament parallel to its theological interpretation of the fall of Jerusalem in 586 BCE as the wholesale punishment of the people by an angry God for their sins. The destruction of the people of God, corresponding to the divine declaration in Amos 8:2 (NRSV), "The end has come upon my people Israel," is never envisioned in the New Testament. True, parallels of sorts with the Christian gospel present themselves, such as the bad news/good news sequence offered in the third poem, while basic truths about God and humanity emerge. Nevertheless, the nearest one can come to such punitive suffering in the New Testament is the loving Father's disciplining in Hebrews 12:5–11, which is borrowed from the wisdom teaching in Proverbs 3:11–12. However, Psalm 89:30–45 trenchantly distinguishes such tough love from the dire calamity that involved the ending of the Davidic monarchy as part of the dismantling of the Judean state.

In the New Testament, especially in Romans 1–8, God's anger rests on sinning humanity as a whole and is to be finally put into operation at the last judgment. However, a favorable verdict has been anticipated for God's people because of the death of Jesus Christ. God has graciously made that provision by which Jesus took their judgment upon himself, and so they no longer face a verdict of condemnation but are set on a Spirit-led road of being right with God. This radical theological realignment puts Lamentations, along with its matching Old Testament material, in a class by itself and not to be directly taken over by Christian readers.

Its pre-Christian content has to be read with theological sensitivity, just as any account of grief has to be read with psychological discernment. Undoubtedly, however, the lessons to be learned are profound and unforgettable.

Certainly the chaplain has to be careful not to jump to conclusions. A call to visit an extremely ill Japanese patient drove that lesson home. From the doorway I saw the aged patient unconscious or just asleep and an Asian lady sitting with bowed head in a lonely vigil. I realized I would be relating to the woman, evidently the patient's wife. As I entered the room, a silly joke came into my mind, and to my horror I found myself telling it to her with a broad grin. She threw back her head and laughed and laughed. "I needed that," she said. "I haven't laughed for a long time." Only then did we get down to serious matters. However, the humor, and the subsequent conversation, left that Japanese American woman fortified to continue her vigil. In spite of the cultural assumptions I initially brought to the visit, I had hit on the right approach. In a similar sort of way, the case study of Lamentations challenges Christian readers to discern its manifold significance aright.

1

First Poem (Lamentations 1)

Grief, Guilt, and the Need for Prayer (1)

In 71 CE the Roman emperor Vespasian celebrated the conquest of the rebellious province of Judea the previous year. The conquest had included the destruction of the Jerusalem temple after a siege of the city. Vespasian issued a special bronze coin to commemorate the victory. The obverse bore the emperor's image, while the reverse depicted a woman representing Judea, sitting disconsolate on the ground under an exotic date palm, with her left hand supporting her bowed head. History was strangely repeating itself. More than six centuries earlier, in 586 BCE, the army of King Nebuchadnezzar of Babylon captured the independence-seeking vassal kingdom of Judah. Jerusalem bore the brunt of the attack and fell after an eighteen-month siege. Life as the Judeans knew it came to an end; many of them were deported. Those left behind grieved, and the five poems of the book of Lamentations are the memento of their grief, with the first two poems portraying a mourning woman, like the one on Vespasian's coin.

This first poem, like the next one, features in the Hebrew an acrostic structure that uses in turn the twenty-two letters of the alphabet at the start of the first word in each stanza. This artistic device that links stanza to stanza not only reveals the dimensions of the poem but also expresses a totality of suffering and grief, from A to Z as it were. What elsewhere in the poem is indicated by the prevalence of *all* and by the cry *Is there any anguish like my anguish?* in the twelfth stanza is more generally conveyed by the methodical, relentless progression through the alphabet. Anyone whose life is filled by grief from horizon to horizon can find fellow feeling here. The metrical structure of the Hebrew poetic lines is also a monument to grief. A significant number of lines reflect a meter of three beats plus two beats, the limping meter used, though not exclusively, for Israel's funeral dirges.

The poem falls into two halves, each consisting of eleven stanzas. The stanzas have three lines (but four in stanza 7, as in stanza 19 of the second poem). The stanzas do not always turn out to be units of thought, nor do the lines. At times the sense spills over or stops short, both signs of the chaos of grief reacting to loss and change. The first half of the poem reports the grief of a woman who has suffered; at the close she twice interrupts with her own words. The second half is almost the opposite: the woman speaks throughout, except for a third-person report about her that occurs in the middle stanza.

Whereas the woman on Vespasian's coin represented captured Judea, this woman personifies the fallen capital, Jerusalem. The poem appears to be part of a dramatic liturgy, which the other poems will continue. Here two speakers give expression to the grief of the shocked community evidently gathered on the ruined temple site in Jerusalem. A description of the memorial service held after the 9/11 collapse of the World Trade Center in New York helps to evoke the scene: "Everyone around me wore the same numb look of grief that I wore. We all looked pale and zombie-like, as though we couldn't quite focus our eyes. . . . To my right I was shocked to see one of the last remaining Trade Center buildings, charred and black. At the street level was a grimy Borders bookstore, dirty posters barely visible through the soot-blackened windows" (Carter 2008, 87–88).

The way the woman addresses Yahweh at the end of the ninth and eleventh stanzas and likewise the reporter in the course of the tenth stanza implies a sacred setting associated with the divine presence, as Rudolph suggested. The descriptions of the woman's grief and her verbal contributions are intended to let the community members hear their own mental pain brought out into the open and to direct their incoherent thoughts and emotions into helpful channels. Such guidance would assist them eventually to come to terms with the catastrophe that had overwhelmed them.

Human Losses (1:1–6)

There is a lot for readers to digest in this poem, as in the others, and it will be less taxing to present the material in appropriate sections. The first half of this poem seems to subdivide after the sixth stanza. The first six stanzas have their own coherence in terms of multiple social losses that involve different groups of people who had earlier defined Jerusalem's life; in the next section, material losses are the subject.

> [1]How terrible that the city sits alone,
>   once so great in population size!
> It has turned into a widow, as it were,
>   once so great compared with other nations.
> The first lady of the provinces
>   has turned into a forced laborer.
>
> [2]She sobs and sobs in the nighttime—
>   tears rest on her cheeks.
> She has no comforter
>   out of all her former allies.

> Her friends all betrayed her,
> > turning into her enemies.

³Judah was exiled after enduring affliction
> and hard labor;
it now sits among other nations.
> It could find "no resting place";
it was constantly caught
> after being chased into tight corners.

⁴The roads to Zion are in mourning,
> now that no pilgrims come for festivals;
all her gates feel devastated.
> Her priests groan,
her girls are grieving,
> while her own reaction is bitter sorrow.

⁵Her foes turned out to "be the head,"
> her enemies the ones safe and sound.
The reason is that Yahweh himself made her suffer
> for her many rebel ways.
Her young children "went away
> as prisoners," driven forward by the foe.

⁶Moreover, Lady Zion lost
> all her majesty.
Her royal officials turned, as it were, into deer
> that cannot find pasture
and so run without strength,
> chased by the hunter.

In the early stages of grief, a bereaved person can only say, "I miss X so much." A sympathetic friend may gently coax him or her to put into words what particular attributes or aspects of the lost individual are pined for. Similarly, in this first section of the poem, the grieving community listens as one of their number articulates their grief as he defines their human losses. He details the ones they miss and the roles those persons no longer play. There is an aura of death about these six stanzas. It is not a literal death but rather the cost of losing a variety of social relationships that were so much a part of the community's identity. Those significant parts of their life died, as it were. This reality is described by Nicholas Wolterstorff, who wrote about burying his son, "I buried myself that warm June day" (1987, 42).

The first word, *ekhah* in Hebrew, traditionally belonged to the funeral dirge and introduced a contrast between a grim present and a good past, a chasm that bereavement had created. Here too it introduces such contrasts. It is a shriek, a scream, "not the kind of scream that comes from fright, but the kind that comes from the deepest grief imaginable. It is a scream that comes when there are no words to express what you feel. . . . It is a scream that rails against logic and fate and everything there is" (Hood 2008, 139). The Hebrew word is generally translated "how" but is better expanded into *How terrible that . . . !* in order to express its emotional intensity. In this case it tells us that the liturgy leader, who here has the role of reporter, is not like a television or radio reporter sent to cover a story and soon to speed away from the scene. He is a member of the mourning community and immersed in the story he tells. His task is to pastorally lead the congregation in giving expression to an overwhelming grief that is equally his own.

In the first line, *sits* describes a mourning posture. A parallel comes from the experience of Nehemiah, who likewise "sat down and wept. For some days I mourned" (Neh. 1:4). The word *alone* sets the tone for this section and summarizes it. So many of the social interactions the community had taken for granted were no more. The bustling metropolis was a ghost town, apart from such gatherings as the present one, for many of the people had been deported. It had lost its greatness twice over, since its international political prestige was also a thing of the past. The comparison with *a widow* has to be understood culturally and sociologically. The word means "a once married woman who has no means of financial support and who is in need of special legal protection." Applied to a city, this term refers to its economic poverty and struggle for survival (Cohen 1973, 77–78). Nor is this a purely ancient or alien phenomenon. Joyce Brothers, in *Widowed*, ruefully refers to widows as "among our country's most oppressed minorities" (1990, 81). Jerusalem's key role among *the provinces* may be gauged from its earlier function as a meeting place for the western states to conspire against Babylon (see the historical details in Jer. 27:3). The order in the contrasts, moving twice from negative to positive and then from positive to negative, means that the first stanza is framed by notes of desolation, as Bergant has observed.

Stanza 2 will eventually expand on this latter social loss, the security of alliance with neighboring states. That security had evaporated as those states had been forced by defeat or intimidation into joining Babylon's side. So Jerusalem had suffered the isolating contrast of enmity after friendship. But this stanza starts with a report of the personified city's extreme grief. The city has been increasingly personified in the course of the first stanza by the use of simile and metaphor. Her distress is evidenced in sobbing aloud that, knowing no bounds, continues into the night. This is a time when, for other people, silence prevails and restorative sleep can be enjoyed, but paradoxically it is a time that provokes grief by its lack of distracting stimulation. "There is nothing to blunt the edge of sorrow or divert attention from it" (Peake 1911, 302).

Especially moving is the visual detail of tears on the cheeks. The visualization adds to the text a dramatic feature that reminds my chaplain self of a custom in the maternity unit of a hospital. Sometimes you see a card taped to the door of a patient's room. On the card is a picture of a fallen green leaf, and resting on the leaf is a glistening dewdrop. It is a symbol of grief, warning the staff that the patient has experienced a miscarriage, a fetal death, or a stillborn delivery. The green leaf fallen prematurely from a tree and the tear-like drop of dew convey grief over a lost potential. Here in this poem, the image of tears on a woman's cheeks gave permission to the hearing congregation to weep and must have made their eyes glisten with their own tears.

Lack of comforters is a somber drumbeat that will be sounded all through the first poem, reflecting the intensity of the grief. Comfort in this poem refers not to the result of bringing about the end of mourning, as in Isaiah 40:1–2, but to the processes of showing emotional identification with those who grieve (Anderson 1991, 84) and of offering positive consolation to them (Olyan 2004, 47–48). Here the lack accentuates the community's isolation. In Israel's world, a strong sense of solidarity usually ensured that family and friends would gather round and minister to the mourner by their presence. So, for example, Job's friends sat on the ground with him in silence for a full week, sharing the numb shock of his initial sorrow (Job 2:13). When bad relationships in the community meant that such comfort was denied and "I have become like a bird alone on a roof," as one psalmist exclaimed (Ps. 102:7), or "no one cares" (Ps. 142:4; cf. Ps. 69:20), the situation was dire indeed. In this case, the people have lost their former allies, and the political reversal has taken an emotional toll.

The list of major social losses goes on. Nothing can make up for them. The community had suffered large-scale deportation to Babylonia. The repetition of *sits* from the first stanza is significant, as Hunter (1996, 105) observes. Qualified with *among other nations*, it spells out the affinity of experience and yet distance between the survivors and the former nation of Judah. *Affliction* is illustrated by the systematic, ruthless rounding up of deportees (Salters 1986, 87). It sounds uncannily like the way the Nazis herded Jews first into ghettos and then into trains that would travel to unknown eastern destinations. In most cases, the people were never to be seen again.

The ache of such a loss cuts savagely across the grain of a long-settled community. It cries out for reflection, for some attempt at explanation. Did such a calamity make any sense, especially as it was believed that God had given the land to Israel as a place of rest? In this case an interpretation could be offered. It is the beginning of a long process of finding meaning for the calamity, a process that will come to fruition only in the positive developments of the third poem. Upon the hectic scenes of Judeans vainly trying to escape the roundup is superimposed a text that the listening congregation, versed in Scripture, would recognize as one of a series of solemn curses for radical national disobedience of God: Deuteronomy 28:65. This curse pronounced "no repose, no resting place for your foot" but instead a fate of being scattered among other nations. The first half of the poem will be increasingly marked by this spiritual agenda. Its purpose is to foster a spirit of repentance and confession among these prodigal sons and daughters left in the land. We readers are not to interpret the agenda as being an all-inclusive explanation of the suffering of believers, for it stands poles apart from the innocent suffering of Job. But it does raise a flag of accountability. It poses a challenge: that victims of suffering may to a lesser or greater degree be victims of their own bad choices. And yet they must not be tempted by this text to take upon themselves the burden of unrealistic guilt.

Stanza 4 registers another loss and contrast, the termination of happy pilgrimage to the festivals on Judah's sacred calendar. *Zion* is here a religious term for Jerusalem as the home of the temple. This term is chosen to fit the new context in this stanza, which now moves away from secular and political perspectives. The empty roads to the desolated shrine and the ruined city gates are personified as themselves in mourning. To grieving eyes, everything around tends to be endued with grief. C. S. Lewis wrote of his wife's death, "Her absence is like the sky, spread over everything" (1976, 24). No longer could be heard the pilgrim's glad cry of anticipation, "I rejoiced with those who said to me, 'Let us go to the house of the LORD,'" or gladder cry of attainment, "Our feet are standing in your gates, O Jerusalem" (Ps. 122:1–2). The festivals' personnel—the priests who organized them and ministered to their joy and the girls who like cheerleaders took part in the religious processions to the temple area (Ps. 68:25)—now mourned their inactivity instead. The sorrow of the woman-city who represents the religious community as a whole is called *bitter*. The term has a parallel in Naomi's cry of anguish in reaction to the deaths of her husband and two sons, "Don't call me Naomi [pleasant]. Call me Marah [bitter]" (Ruth 1:20).

The fifth stanza returns to the theological theme broached in the third. The reporter develops his role of interpreter. The stanza is framed by two more quotations from Deuteronomy 28 (vv. 44 and 41 respectively), while the middle sentence preaches its message. The relevance of the quotations to the context of present grief is that they match the mention of enemies in the second stanza and of deportation in the third. There is an implicit contrast in the first citation. God's people had forfeited the blessing of being "the head and not the tail" and "at the top, never at the bottom" (Deut. 28:13) and had gotten the opposite. The motif of deportation is given extra poignancy by the text's specification of saying a permanent good-bye to the younger generation. The community's spiritual contribution to the calamity is now identified as *many rebel ways*, for which they were providentially held accountable. The tragedy of 586 BCE is bluntly placed in the echo chamber of Deuteronomy 28, which may have been read at the service. The *rebel ways* are not spelled out, and the imposing tradition of the Law—"the commands and decrees" given by Yahweh (Deut. 28:15, 45)—on the one hand and the consciences of the listening community on the other were meant to supply the lack. The appeal to Scripture brought meaning to the mental chaos that grief so often entails, but at the cost of taking responsibility for their abandonment of covenant obligations. Judah's rebellion against Nebuchadnezzar that was the political cause of exile is supplied with a counterpart, a spiritual rebellion against their God, and the doom of Deuteronomy 28 is claimed as a fitting reprisal from the Lord of history.

The term *Zion*, used religiously in the fourth stanza, has a royal connotation in the sixth. "I have installed my king on Zion," Yahweh once said (Ps. 2:6). Jerusalem had been the age-old royal capital of the Davidic dynasty. Now that distinguished role had been lost, and the king was, in fact two kings were, languishing in Babylon. Psalm 89 reveals how deeply that loss was felt. An ignominious vignette is supplied of the once powerful palace officials, veterans of stable government, feebly trying to scurry away after the siege and the starvation it entailed, just like a herd of weakened, ill-nourished deer.

For the first of many times in the book there occurs the title *Lady Zion*, sometimes *Lady Jerusalem*. Literally "daughter Zion," the term has plausibly been interpreted as painting a picture of civilized stability, since daughters are associated with building up society from its center, the home (Follis 1992, 1103). It has an ironic ring of former security in the book, as in Isaiah 1:8, which reinforces the sense of loss by turning its security upside down (Labahn 2003, 66).

This first section of six stanzas has two purposes, a major one and a minor one in terms of allocated space. The major purpose is that it articulates the grief of a barely surviving community with an emotional analysis of their plight in terms of the loss of different parts of their support system. Both tears and talking have encouraged the community members to confront their grief. The minor purpose is to broach another agenda, to involve them in a service of confession and repentance by interpreting their tragedy in moral and spiritual terms as the providential work of God, by appealing to Deuteronomy 28. This second purpose will be developed in the next section. Grief eventually has to come to terms with reality, and in this case there was a spiritual reality for which the grieving community had to make room before they could embrace a new and positive future.

Material Losses (1:7–11)

The second section that concludes the first half of the poem consists of flashbacks. *Remembered* appropriately announces this feature. Such intrusive memories were certainly a component of the first section, where the text went to and fro, from a grief-filled present to past suffering. The flashbacks, suggesting what modern people know as post-traumatic stress disorder (PTSD), take over the text, except for the cries of prayer that unexpectedly close stanzas 9 and 11.

> ⁷Jerusalem remembered
>   during her affliction and wandering
> all the valuables
>   that had once been hers before.
> When her people fell into the hands of the foe
>   and she had no helper,
> the foes gloated over her, laughing
>   at her destruction.
>
> ⁸Jerusalem committed sin—
>   that's why she became an object of mockery.
> All who once respected her came to despise her,
>   seeing her naked.
> She could only groan
>   and turn away.
>
> ⁹Evidence of her impurity was there on her skirt.
>   She never thought about the consequences
> and had an astounding downfall,
>   but had no comforter.
> "Look, Yahweh, at my affliction,
>   how arrogantly the enemy acted!"
>
> ¹⁰The foe stretched out his hand
>   to grab all her valuables.
> She even saw members of other nations
>   entering her sanctuary—
> those whom you had given orders
>   not to "enter" your "assembly."

41

[11]All her people were groaning
    as they searched for bread.
They offered their valuables in return for food
    to restore their vitality.
"Look, Yahweh, and take notice
    how despicable I have become!"

Apart from the cries at the end of this section, the present fades into unreality. "Loss creates a barren present, as if one were sailing on a vast sea of nothingness. Those who suffer loss . . . want to return to the harbor of the past and recover what was lost. . . . Memories of the past only remind them of what they have lost" (Sittser 1996, 56). The memories were not only of the good old days but also of the catastrophe that had struck them from the regular calendar. These memories are constantly revisited in this section, as the liturgy leader seems to read the minds of the listening congregation.

Whereas the earlier section dwelt on the loss of social status and roles, this one concentrates on material losses. So many things, like so many people, were no longer there. Kübler-Ross and Kessler rightly say to the one who grieves, "It is a tremendous and heartrending adjustment you must make to a new world full of losses" (2005, 77). Now the congregation pines for their other type of loss, which a repeated keyword, *valuables*, indicates (stanzas 7, 10, and 11). One may talk abstractly and glibly about bondage to things, and indeed this can be a spiritual danger. However, cherished possessions become an embodiment of ourselves, an extension of our personalities, and so after their loss they are sorely missed. Possessions hold intimate memories and are part of who we are. If a home is burglarized and items are stolen or the house ransacked, the homeowner feels personally violated. The fall season in southern California brings brush fires that can completely destroy adjacent homes. The TV news shows heartbreaking cameos of people standing alongside blackened ruins, who say they have lost everything except the clothes they are wearing. In this case the material loss was aggravated by *affliction*, which is explained in the latter half of the seventh stanza as not only a lack of humanitarian help from ethnic neighbors but also their callous reaction of ridicule, which at a secondary stage rubbed salt into emotional wounds. For instance, Ezekiel 25:6 records about the Ammonites that "you clapped your hands and stamped your feet, rejoicing with all the malice of your heart" in response to Judah's experience in 586 BCE. To what does *wandering* refer? "It is common," says a grief manual, "for the bereaved to be very restless, to wander anxiously" as they pine and search for those they have lost (Rando 1984, 33).

"Serves you right!" is never a welcome retort to hear from other people, but here the reporter frankly declares there was some truth in the observation, a truth that the surviving community had eventually to own up to. Nevertheless, it is sympathetically admitted that the humiliation was keenly felt, especially as it reversed earlier respect. Loss of dignity is always a cruel experience. Stripped of earlier assets, the community shivered in shame. They could not evade it: *She could only groan and turn away.* The emotional pain was an all-engrossing reality. "Turning inward in grief . . . is necessary because the intense feelings are all an individual can bear. Interacting with [others] can quickly become too much for an already overloaded emotional circuit" (Mitchell and Anderson 1983, 93).

The ninth stanza starts by returning to the truth first mentioned in stanza 8 but puts it in a metaphorical form. The metaphor draws on the gender of the woman-city that stood for the grieving community. Not that the menstrual blood staining her clothing was ever regarded in literal terms of moral sin, but it did cause ritual impurity (Lev. 15:19–24; 18:19). In turn, this impurity could be used as a figurative illustration of wrongdoing outside the limited world of taboos, as Ezekiel 36:17 says.

Having lived in the moment, the community had been unprepared for the wages that sin inexorably pays (cf. Deut. 32:29; Isa. 47:7). In this case it was the *astounding downfall* of capital and country. They had forgotten a basic rule of life that can be simply expressed in terms of a rule for the motorist: don't just look at the car in front of you and at the immediate stretch of road, but look much farther ahead and anticipate any changes looming on the road you're taking. The catastrophe that occurred came as an incredible shock, but in rueful retrospect it had its own logic, like a serious accident after an evening of carefree drinking.

So far this section, begun in the seventh stanza, has moved a long way, from memories of national loss to a description of the affliction that accompanied such loss, to the humiliation involved in that affliction, and then to the moral responsibility that the community had to assume in dealing with the affliction, in contrast to their earlier irresponsibility. The text will move to other examples of material loss in the next two stanzas but with a significant shift of thinking.

Within the next stanzas, there are three surprises. First, a new voice breaks into the reporter's monologue at the end of the ninth and eleventh stanzas. The woman-city that represents the listening congregation as its role model is suddenly given her own voice as a prelude to her speaking her mind throughout the second half of the poem. In the cultural background lies the close association of women with mourning. Professional women mourners had the task of leading a family or community in expressing grief. It is likely that in the liturgical service a professional mourner played her role. Unexpectedly, however, she utters not a funeral dirge, as a woman mourner normally would, but a lament prayer to God.

This is the second surprise: for the first time Yahweh is addressed directly. Hitherto the poem's horizon has been limited to the dirge, a prayer-less cry that has the enormously useful advantage of engaging in a grieving description of radical change from a positive past to a negative present—negative reactions were all that the congregation could be expected to express at this early stage. The only theological note has been imported from the equally negative Deuteronomy 28, which was quoted and applied to the tragedy in 586 BCE, along with its motifs of divine curses realized against a sinful people. The ground covered by the first section has not been significantly advanced by the second one so far.

But now a new factor emerges. The congregation can pray! The text uses dramatic interruption by a hitherto silent character to enhance this new possibility. The possibility is intended as a model for the congregation to follow. Much later, in the fifth and final poem, they will do so. The prayer model draws on the tradition of the communal and individual laments in the book of Psalms, which are able to tell the same story of misery as the dirge, but in a context of prayer to God and as a prelude to touching God's heart and eventually finding divine resources to transcend tragedy.

And so the text can spring a third surprise for the reader. Positive expectations can be entertained, even if barely positive at first. The barometer that registers the national mood can start edging toward a brighter prospect. The text has introduced a turning point. It is a literary turning point that has to do with possibility. The new voice that pleads for divine favor not only does so in a staccato way but is just a stage voice; the congregation has yet to translate possibility into reality.

Of the three surprises, the most important for the book is the broaching of prayer. The congregated people were unable to pray at the moment and for a long time to come, but to hear their imaginary counterpart doing so must have moved them and brought an unexpected glimmer to their eyes. In my chaplaincy work, new patients who have requested a visit are asked to specify their spiritual needs, if they so wish. In response, patients most often single out prayer when they return their referral forms. The patients, however devout they are, find they no longer have any energy to find the words for prayer now that they are beset by illness. They can only let their individual stories, often a recital of negative experiences, tumble out jerkily to my listening ear. It is my privilege to translate their heartfelt troubles, one by one, into a litany of prayer. Their sincere *amen* tells me their deep appreciation of what they could no longer and not yet do for themselves. They regard it, and rightly so, as one of the steps toward recovery. In similar fashion, an implicit bridge is built in this text between the old and new perspectives on the catastrophe of 586 BCE. It concerns the specific nature of Zion's suffering. It is viewed with a deep sense of divine providence, which was earlier in evidence as a reaction to Judah's rebelliousness. Ultimately, such a powerful God is the only one who can radically change things and bring about a fresh start of any kind (Hunter 1996, 145–46). So prayer to God is the only way forward. God is the only one who can fix the problem.

The stanza divisions do not quite accord here with the demarcation of thought. Hunter (1996, 130) has rightly grouped together the seven lines that begin and end with the petitions that close stanzas 9 and 11, while Westermann has recognized that the petitions act as an outer frame for what lies between. Moreover, the tenth stanza expounds Zion's first petition, and the first two lines of the eleventh expound her second one. The petitions are integrated into the context by the reporter's resuming his third-person narration and defining the petitions' content in terms of the earlier motif of lost *valuables*. The call *Look* functions as an appeal for compassion, for which we may compare Psalm 9:13, "O LORD, see how my enemies persecute me! Have mercy."

Earlier, *affliction* had been the reporter's word for the catastrophe in terms of the emotional sufferings caused by loss of freedom (stanza 3) and by crushing humiliation (stanza 7). Now it features in an accusation of the victors' arrogance. More literally, they had acted big, throwing their weight around. The focus veers from the victims to the invaders, and the invaders' own wrongdoing is brought to God's scrutiny. In the prophetic tradition of the Old Testament, the relationship between divine providence and human history is admitted to be complex. A military defeat might well be defined in terms of moral punishment so that the adversary is God's ally. But that is not necessarily the end of the matter. War is a dirty business that leaves nobody's hands clean. As Reinhold Niebuhr wrote of Lincoln's problems in dealing with slavery, "The drama of history is shot through with moral meaning; but the meaning is never exact. Sin and punishment, virtue and reward are never precisely proportioned" (1964, 74).

In Israel's case the invaders were liable to show an excess of violence that went far beyond the divine will for justice, and so they became culpable in turn. Isaiah 10:5–19 is the classic exposition of this complex tradition, while Isaiah 47:6 says it succinctly. Here a window is opened a little toward this tradition—it will be opened wider at the end of the poem. It is made the basis of a minimal appeal for divine attention and empathy. Sinners though they were, the people of Judah were not to be identified totally with their sin but needed compassion as well as blame, though it is much easier, for humans at least, to be compassionate in the case of innocent suffering.

In the appeal for compassion, the text has just crossed a psychological and theological line, a first but firm step that the rest of the book will continue to take. For the listening congregation, it would not have been a difficult step because it implicitly appealed to their sense of resentful grievance and acknowledged it as justified in the bigger scheme of things. There are situations of grievance where "anger, like sorrow, at the horror of suffering is a necessary prerequisite to being able to resist suffering" (Dobbs-Allsopp 2002, 73). Such grievance had to be voiced, and the voicing would nudge a shocked and resenting clientele forward for their own good. And giving to the woman-city that was their alter ego her own voice to express their grievance brings some salve to this particular wound of grief.

There is a severe type of grief that comes with a second wound, the wound of grievance, attached to it. Mourning for a little girl is aggravated if she died on the way to the hospital after being caught in the crossfire of rival gangs in Los Angeles. Or if a beloved grandfather passes away unexpectedly in a nursing home and the family suspects that neglect or abuse accelerated his death. Or if a woman walking legitimately across an intersection, shopping bag in hand, is fatally struck down by a hit-and-run driver. In such cases a family representative is interviewed, tearfully pleading for a thorough investigation and for justice to be done, and people's hearts are touched. It is this sort of grievance that animates Zion's prayer and screams out for satisfaction.

In the tenth stanza, the reporter in a flashback gives a notorious example of enemy arrogance. The enemy's grabbing hands had violated the sanctity of the temple and stolen its treasures that were part of Zion's *valuables*. The crime is presented in terms of eyewitness evidence—helpless spectators could only watch with horror. It is typical of psalm laments to cite enemy excess as motivation for an appeal to God, as Psalms 75:4–7 and 79:1 illustrate. Once more an element of psalm laments is used. Almost unconsciously the reporter slips into Zion's prayer mode and turns to protest to the God present at the ruined sacred site where the liturgical ceremony is being held. Trespass by foreigners was a violation of God's Torah. This is what one could extrapolate from Deuteronomy 23:3, though worship had been far from the aliens' minds. If earlier in the poem Deuteronomy 28 pointed an accusing finger at the victims, so virtually did Deuteronomy 23 at the victors! This pagan trespass into Zion's sanctuary was an affront that must surely touch God's heart in her favor. It constitutes a grievance against Judah's enemies and so paves the way for Zion's later prayer of grievance in stanzas 21 and 22 that expands her initial prayer in stanza 9.

The third case of *valuables* in this section occurs in an advance explanation of Zion's second appeal. This flashback goes further back, to the long siege after food supplies started running out. Once more there was loss that led to grief, loss first of food and then of valuables with which people tried to buy food. In 1722, during the six-month siege of Isfahan, capital of Persia, by an Afghan army, women handed over their pearls and jewels for food until even precious stones could not buy bread (Lawler 2009, 44). A similar example comes from a teaching trip I made to St. Petersburg at the end of 1997, a period of economic stringency in Russia. Social security checks were not being paid to the elderly, and there was much unemployment. Walking one Saturday afternoon down Nevsky Prospekt, the city's Rodeo Drive, I saw old and middle-aged people trying to sell cherished heirlooms to passersby in order to survive, and my heart went out to them. It is such a grief-laden situation, but very much worse, that underlies Zion's second appeal. An appeal to God based on personal or national suffering is another feature of psalm laments; Psalm 123:4 is a near parallel. In the present context there is an echo of the secondary despising mentioned in the eighth stanza; in both places feeling despised is associated with the loss of assets. The hope is that God would be stirred to compassion.

Like the first section of the poem, this second section has concentrated on loss and grief and on the guilt that underlay it in this case. But the loss of material rather than social attachments has been in view. A new element is the two appeals to God presented at the close. They are cries for divine attention, which are motivated by grievance. In Judah's case the grievance was enemy aggression, which had generated emotional suffering. Zion's voice is made to honor this grievance that was a firm part of the listening congregation's grief. The appeals based on aggression and suffering both draw on the tradition of psalm laments. However, the first one also draws on the prophetic tradition of the arrogant enemy who goes beyond the divine mandate and should suffer in turn. Would God be stirred to do something? Nobody knew, but prayer was the only possible way forward. Perhaps Exodus 3:7 would come true again: "The LORD said, 'I have indeed seen the misery of my people . . . and I am concerned about their suffering.'" One could only pray, but pray one must.

Zion's Cry of Culpability (1:12–16)

The second half of this poem is a repetition of the first half—grief is by its nature repetitive. This second half too expresses grief, guilt, and a need for prayer but in more passionate tones. The woman-city's voice now takes over rather than interrupts, while the reporter has an interrupter's role in the middle stanza. Her feminine voice brings with it shrillness and emotional intensity. This half of the poem falls into two equal parts, each consisting of five stanzas, while in between the reporter gives an authoritative comment on Zion's two contributions. As in the first half, the overall thrust is the articulation of grief, the interpretation of this particular grief, and making a forward move by means of prayer. The aim, as before, is to help the listening community by empathy, spiritual analysis, and even constructiveness of a preliminary kind. Perhaps the most significant aspect of the second half is that the woman-city endorses the reporter's perspectives. This endorsement is important because she represents a role model for the listening congregation to follow. They are nudged toward affirming these perspectives as their own by the more personal tones of Zion's testimony.

> [12]Should it not be your concern, all you passersby?
>   Take notice and look!
>   Is there any anguish like my anguish,
>   which was inflicted on me,
>   me whom Yahweh made to suffer
>   on his day of burning anger?

¹³From above he sent a fire
    into my bones, and it raged there.
He spread a net for my feet.
    He turned me back.
He left me feeling devastated
    and sick all the time.

¹⁴My rebel ways were tied into a yoke,
    interwoven by his own hands.
They were mounted on my neck;
    it sapped my energy.
The Lord handed me over
    to those I could not resist.

¹⁵The Lord, setting no value
    on all the stalwart troops I had within my walls,
rallied an army against me
    to defeat my soldiers.
The Lord trod the winepress
    of the young Lady Judah.

¹⁶Those are the reasons why I am sobbing,
    why water streams from my eyes, these eyes of
        mine,
having no comforter close at hand
    to restore my vitality.
My children feel devastated
    that the enemy has prevailed.

In terms of analysis of the poem, the first half focused on a
negative spiritual interpretation of the catastrophe by citing the
sinister language of Deuteronomy 28 and urging that it had a counterpart in Judah's experience. Not unexpectedly, the woman-city
will echo the reporter's appeal to Deuteronomy 28 by repeating in
the eighteenth stanza a quotation from it found in the fifth. More
generally she endorses the reporter's statement *Yahweh made her
suffer* in the fifth stanza by saying that *Yahweh made me suffer* in
the twelfth. However, the analysis in the second half will mostly
rely on another tradition, on features of the tradition of preexilic

prophecy, in order to interpret the catastrophe and to begin to move beyond it. Readers will recall that the prophetic understanding of a tension between deserved providential misfortune and the culpability of its human agents was used in the ninth stanza to support a call to prayer. Now different prophetic elements are introduced. Accordingly, the total effect of the first poem, in terms of spiritual interpretation, is that the Law, to which Deuteronomy belongs, and the Prophets are claimed to be fulfilled by the catastrophe in 586 BCE.

One of the new prophetic components comes in the form of bookends that provide its focus. Stanza 12 refers to the tradition of the day of the Lord (or day of Yahweh) when it mentions *his day of burning anger*, while stanza 21 will refer to another aspect of that fateful day. The other prophetic component lies more in the background but, once noticed, can be seen to have a dominant role. The woman-city's first outburst concentrates on the catastrophe as Yahweh's work of grim intervention, while her second outburst focuses on the human outworking of that intervention. Similarly, the reporter's commentary in the middle (stanza 17) highlights both elements by not only echoing the first element but also anticipating the second. Those who have read the prophetic books of the Old Testament can recognize in these elements staple ingredients of the announcements of disaster that crowd their pages. The announcements define coming disaster in a twofold way, as divine intervention and its human consequences. Amos 8:11–12, a typical example, moves from "I will send a famine" to "Men will stagger from sea to sea." Such hostile divine intervention is also encountered in the Psalms, but it is much more characteristic of the prophetic books.

The prophetic announcement of disaster presupposes the guilt of the victims. It is common to express that guilt as a preparatory reason for disaster, and reason and announcement together make up a prophetic oracle of disaster, as in Hosea 2:5–7, which first cites Israel's wrongdoing before specifying God's intervention and its consequences. Here in Lamentations, references to guilt are not lacking in the second half of the poem, as in the first half. They show up in the admissions of stanzas 14 and 18. The ultimate point of the prophetic books was to interpret 586 BCE in such providential terms of reprisal for wrongdoing. The book of Lamentations adds its own amen to this interpretation. Here the woman-city's voice continues to articulate the congregation's grief and leads them into further analysis and confession. Readers may compare Lamentations' amen with Isaiah 42:24–25, which in a shorter span makes a similar interpretive claim that Yahweh was responsible for Judah's tragic end, reacting to their sinning by pouring out on them "his burning anger, the violence of war."

A bird's-eye view of Zion's first outburst would see it as announcing the *anguish* that *Yahweh made* Zion *suffer* in the opening stanza, defining it in the next three, and giving it as the reason for Zion's grieving in the closing one. Talk and tears are featured once more. Most of the section is devoted to Zion's telling her story, now from a new angle. Over and over again grieving persons need to tell their stories, reliving aspects of them in flashbacks. Each story comes with the implicit plea, "Don't stop me even if you've heard this one." Here the character of the woman-city uses the story she tells to stimulate the congregation's own grief, even as she reminds them of the woeful messages of the preexilic prophets and claims that those messages have come true in the congregation's experience.

In stanza 12, the initial appeal is an indirect allusion to Zion's plight and her craving for comfort. A scenario occasionally described in the Old Testament (e.g., 1 Kings 9:8–9; Jer. 19:8; 22:8–9), one that must have been commonplace in the ancient world, portrays travelers passing by a city once vibrant with life but now destroyed by enemy attack. They stand and look at the ruins with curious horror and then pass on, shaking their heads in shock. A contemporary scenario is the way drivers on the freeway slow down to look with horrified fascination at the result of a tragic accident. Here Zion puts herself in the ancient scenario, as she will later, in Lamentations 2:15. She pleads for some feelings of humanity to be shown by these imaginary travelers, though she knows the stereotyped scenario is not scripted that way. Still, she pleads for empathy and tells her story as intently as did the ancient mariner in Coleridge's poem, who clutched the lapels of the wedding guest with his skinny hand. Zion's story is a story of excruciating suffering; it felt as bad as any suffering could be. "From her position inside the pain, no one has suffered as much as she because there is no way she could imagine more suffering" (O'Connor 2002, 26).

Zion draws on the longstanding prophetic tradition of the day of the Lord. It is featured, for example, in Amos 5:18–20 and in Isaiah 2:12–18, while it is the theme of Zephaniah 1:2–2:3, where it is closely associated with divine wrath and anger, as here and in Ezekiel 7:5–9. In the prophetic books, the day of the Lord is a day of doom for God's people; it takes on a canonical function as a premonition of Judah's fate in 586 BCE. Accordingly, Ezekiel 13:5, especially in the NJPS version, which clearly brings out its past perspective, and Ezekiel 34:12 can look back on that fate as the manifestation of the day of the Lord, as the woman-city does here.

The suffering is described in the next three stanzas as hammer blows wielded by none other than Israel's own God. These blows echo the prophetic announcements of disaster that envision Yahweh's forceful intervention into the lives of the covenant people, initiating destruction. What was future in those announcements is now history. Traditional prophetic language is reused. Sending fire was a way that Amos described divine intervention; it is used as a refrain in Amos 1:3–2:5, "I will send a fire." Here it is a particular outworking of *his day of burning anger*. It is integrated with the imagery of the woman-city and described as a raging fever, fire in her very bones, like the fever of Psalm 102:3. Switching analogies, that day was also like the hunter's net that trapped its victims. The lament psalms use this analogy to refer to human enemies, but the prophets used it of God's future judgment (e.g., Hosea 7:12). While most sufferers will not easily relate to these analogies, they can to the motif of being turned back. Grief of all kinds comes crashing into human life, sets up roadblocks, and brings to a shuddering halt the ongoing journey of life. We are left wondering when and even whether we will ever get back on track. We can also identify with the emotional turmoil of the final line.

Why had Yahweh made Zion suffer? The first two lines of stanza 14 justify the divine intervention with an allusion to the way the prophets regularly diagnosed the people's moral and spiritual condition before issuing a prognosis of disaster. In the present context, Zion endorses the reporter's reference to *her rebel ways* in the fifth stanza, after earlier echoing his reference to Yahweh's making her suffer in the same stanza. The imagery of the yoke finely illustrates the moral process of cause and effect operating by divine agency. Zion's *rebel ways* led to consequences at God's hands, those ways being fabricated as it were into a heavy yoke that pressed down hard on Zion's shoulders and left her exhausted. The weight of the load being pulled or carried was experienced through the yoke. Any grieving person can identify with this image of grief as a heavy burden that drains all energy.

The repercussion of *rebel ways* colors the remaining three vignettes of the divine intervention. These three statements all have as their subject *the Lord*, which is not to be confused with "the Lord," typically used in English versions to render the divine name, Yahweh. God's people had rebelled against their lord and master in the covenant relationship (cf. Mal. 1:6). "God's authority and (superior) power are allowed to dominate" (Renkema 1998, 167). By this means a link between divine activity and Zion's accountability is maintained. The three statements gradually increase in providential intensity, from Yahweh's permitting defeat, to rallying the defeating army, to single-handedly carrying out the massacre that represented the catastrophe in 586 BCE. The image of the bloodbath, which is developed from treading red grapes, is portrayed even more gruesomely in a later prophetic text (Isa. 63:3–6) and echoed in the New Testament (Rev. 14:19–20; 19:15).

The closing stanza reacts to the divine intervention with profound grief, first reverting to the sobbing reported in the second stanza and then, as there, complaining of the absence of comforters. Repetition is necessary, and never vain, for those who grieve. The potential of comfort to *restore vitality* repeats the description of another of life's staples, food, in the eleventh stanza. Comfort from another person, with its warm energy, can assuage the pain of grief and bring back flickers of life, but Zion is aware she has no such resource, and the knowledge intensifies her grief.

The final line of the stanza opens a door to Zion's next outburst by referring to the human repercussions of Yahweh's intervention, here in terms of *the enemy*. She also dramatically embraces the listening congregation as *my children*, speaking of their resentment and indignation in reaction to their victorious human foes. "This too is part of my distress, as I will go on to explain," she affirms, while implicitly urging that they should endorse her spiritual interpretation of the tragedy.

Comments on Zion's Cries (1:17)

While Zion sits sobbing for a while, the reporter takes the opportunity to reflect on and reinforce her words, spoken and yet to be spoken.

> [17]Zion stretches out her hands
>   but has no comforter.
> Yahweh ordered Jacob's foes
>   to surround it.
> Jerusalem became
>   something impure in the middle of them.

At this structural midpoint of the second half of the poem, the reporter first dwells on Zion's unmet craving for comfort, evidenced in the reaching out of stanza 12 and in her negative statements in stanza 16 and later in stanza 21. Perhaps implicitly listeners and readers are being prepared for the particular comfort to be found eventually in God through reaching out in prayer. Then the reporter sums up the two all-important ingredients of the prophetic program of disaster, the divine intervention and the human consequences of defeat and loss. He advocates the relevance of this twofold program for understanding Jerusalem's fall. God's *orders* referred to the Torah in stanza 10, but here the prophetic revelation is in view, as later in the second poem (stanza 17) and the third (line 37). In that revelation, Yahweh's negative will was disclosed. Linafelt (2000, 41, 157), comparing Numbers 19:11–20, has suggested that the metaphor of impurity in this case has in view a defiling corpse. Zion was left for dead and even despised and shunned as she suffered. Suffering may be augmented by the stigma an objective loss sometimes brings in its train, such as the humiliation that divorce or loss of one's job or house can carry. The poems of Lamentations have much to say about this secondary factor of humiliation, which is "a lingering and excruciating pain persisting in the form of shame and reproach after the first distresses of the siege and destruction had subsided" (Gottwald 1954, 75).

Zion's Confession and Prayer of Grievance (1:18–22)

Zion describes the outworking of Yahweh's justified intervention in terms of her human losses, the story of which she retells, and then turns to a grievance she feels needs to be redressed.

> [18]Yahweh is the one in the right,
> because I defied (the words of) his mouth.
> Listen, peoples everywhere,
> and look at my anguish!

My boys and girls
"went away as prisoners."

¹⁹When I called on my allies,
they let me down,
My priests and elders
expired in the city
as they searched for food for themselves
to restore their vitality.

²⁰Look, Yahweh, how troubled I am.
It has become a gut-wrenching experience for
me.
My heart is agitated inside my breast.
Because of my utter defiance
outside the sword brought bereavement,
while inside there was virtual death.

²¹Listen to my groaning—
I have no comforter.
My enemies all cheered on hearing of my bad fate,
as something you yourself had brought about.
May you bring that day which you have announced,
so they become like me!

²²Let all their own bad behavior be brought to your
attention,
and inflict on them
the like of what you inflicted on me
in return for all my rebel ways.
The reason is that I groan so much
and am so sick at heart.

The nature of Zion's human losses as the just outworking of
Yahweh's intervention is explained in the first line. Zion keeps
firmly in mind the providential interpretation of suffering as an
outcome of her waywardness. She has been in the wrong, and so
Yahweh is the one in the right. In other Scriptures—Exodus 9:27;
Ezra 9:15; and Nehemiah 9:33—the two statements stand together
explicitly. Her earlier outburst was directed not against Yahweh

but against the dreadful mistakes she had made in her life, which had set in motion the avalanche of just retribution she experienced. Her defiance of Yahweh's mouth seems to refer to breaking the Law, especially as the stanza goes on to repeat Deuteronomy 28:41 from the fifth stanza.

Then the woman-city repeats her wild appeal of stanza 12, now addressed to the world, to everybody, to anybody, in a search for empathy from some listening ear. Does *peoples* also point to the perceived enormity of her grief? As it fills the mental horizon of grieving Zion, so surely it must that of a much wider audience and can only be breaking news for all of them, as it always was for her. Zion expands upon her *anguish* in the following lines and stanzas, in human terms rather than the divine ones she used earlier. The expression of grief is largely a series of flashbacks readers have been told about before, in the first half of the poem. For those who grieve, but not for their regular hearers, the old story is ever new, always filling their consciousness and needing to be told once more, as intensely as it was the first time. Patience is the prime virtue that empathy requires.

In stanza 19 Zion thinks particularly of key parts of the support system she has lost, the allies who once rallied round her and, at home, those venerable figures of religious and civil authority on whom she leaned. They too had gone, victims of the starvation that had stalked the besieged city of Jerusalem. Who was left to turn to? Only the God on whom she had once relied. As at the close of the first half of the poem, Zion leads the way for the congregation to turn to God by her own appeal for divine empathy, pleading first her bitter grief in terms of its psychosomatic ravages. Then she pleads the suffering the enemy campaign had brought, in terms of the heavy toll of casualties on Judah's battlefields and of the rigors undergone in the besieged capital, which had brought every survivor to death's door, like the psalmist's experience in Psalm 88:3–5. But the grim memories are grounded in the regretful confession that Zion brings to her God, echoing the reference to defiance that opened the eighteenth stanza.

In the last two stanzas Zion turns to God in a prayer for a listening ear, after the plea for a compassionate eye in stanza 20. At last Zion hopes for comfort she had failed to find elsewhere. The woman-city returns to the motif of the day of the Lord broached in the twelfth stanza. In the prophetic literature, the day of the Lord is not presented as a time of coming doom simply for Israel, but it sweeps into its scope neighboring nations who had gone down their own deviant paths and deserved providential retribution from the Lord of the world. The book of Zephaniah bears eloquent testimony to this broader aspect of the day. Here Zion's grievance comes to the fore. Recalling this feature of the prophetic tradition, she pleads that, if justice is to be fully done, the other nations involved in the debacle deserve the day to dawn in their experience also.

As at the close of the first half of the poem, readers can hear articulated the resentful feelings of victims of cruel oppression. They cry out for a Nuremberg-like day of reckoning. Similarly, but with greater assurance, Paul told a group of persecuted Christians that God would "pay back trouble to those who trouble you" in a coming "day" when "the Lord Jesus" would irrupt into the human scene as vindicator of his oppressed people and judge of their oppressors (2 Thess. 1:6–10). Here the offense that is singled out may seem a comparatively minor one, but ridicule can bite deeper into the human psyche than many a physical blow. Stanza 22 picks up the complaint of stanza 7, but doubtless that of stanza 10 also is not far from view. There is an ironic accusation of divine discrimination until fair play is seen to be done. Just as Zion's *rebel ways* brought about her *bad fate*, so the other nations' gamut of *bad behavior* warranted comeuppance. As Nägelsbach, Keil, and Reyburn observe, the final line is meant as backing for the whole appeal begun with *Listen to my groaning* in stanza 21. Zion's groans, evidence of an aching heart, would, she hoped, reach God's compassionate heart.

What has been the role assigned to Zion in this poem? She has endeavored to lead the congregation forward by not only giving expression to their grief but also directing them by means of interpretation toward confession of underlying guilt and encouraging a new, honest openness to God. To this end, the community's resentful feelings of anger have been channeled into a prayer for justice with the aid of a theological tradition learned from the preexilic prophets. The overall analysis offered by Zion and the reporter in the first poem fundamentally depends on applying to the catastrophe of 586 BCE stern lessons drawn from the Law and the Prophets. Such preaching must have been a bitter pill to swallow, but it was intended to lead to eventual healing. In spirit the good folk of Alcoholics Anonymous are a contemporary Zion and her reporter, endeavoring to reach out in rigorous compassion to victims of a different sort of affliction by urging them to take responsibility for their behavior, as a first step toward receiving help from a Higher Power.

2

Second Poem (Lamentations 2)

Grief, Guilt, and the Need for Prayer (2)

The second poem revisits ground already covered in the first one but does so even more passionately (Wiesmann 1926, 158–59). If the latter half of the first poem replayed the earlier half in a higher emotional key, the pattern is intensified here. Three persons dominate the poem. Yahweh, the subject of a barrage of grim verbs in the storytelling of the first eight stanzas, is portrayed awesomely as a giant figure, a personification of negative power. The reporter, who takes over again from Zion as the main speaker, emerges as a character in his own right when, caught up in the story he is telling, he poignantly expresses his personal grief (stanzas 11–13). Moreover, he addresses Zion as *you* (stanzas 13–19). Zion breaks into prayer (stanzas 20–22), addressing Yahweh as *you* and as the subject of sinister verbs, and so these closing stanzas are a counterpart to the dynamic first part of the poem. The personal dimension and the direct interchanges of one individual to another—the reporter turning to Zion and addressing her and Zion holding up her hands and addressing the distinctly characterized God—raise the poem's emotional level and so stimulate the listeners to take its message seriously.

Grief still plays a dominant role in this second poem, and necessarily so, since grief filled the listening congregation's hearts and needed to be brought out into the open. Guilt reappears, but mainly from a different perspective, as readers will observe. The need for prayer is given a larger focus than in the first poem. Why is this? And what is the overall relationship between the two poems? To answer these questions, it is helpful to compare two passages from a prophetic book, Joel 1 and Joel 2:1–17. There, locust plagues over at least two seasons and an accompanying drought threatened the Judean community with extinction. In Joel 1, the prophet encourages the people to resort to the temple for prayer to God, so dire is their crisis. In Joel 2:1–17, the prophet intensifies his appeal by raising the emotional temperature with lurid descriptions of the locusts in terms of the day of the Lord. He presents God in a threatening mode by interpreting the natural disasters as the divine means of judging a sinful people, before encouraging them to flock to the temple for national prayers of repentance. The presentation of God in Joel 2:1–11 is deliberately frightening. I remember that, while writing a commentary on Joel (1976, 64–76), I spent a day working through these verses and that night had a nightmare, so deeply had the text etched itself on my mind. There is a similar persuasive rhetoric in the sequence of the first two poems of Lamentations. The three goals of the initial poem—articulating grief, helping the community take responsibility for their shortcomings by means of spiritual interpretation, and helping members turn in prayer back to God as the only one who could take them beyond their catastrophe—are repeated in the second poem but at a more emotive and strident level in order to drive these messages home and encourage the community to turn to God in their own prayer.

The expression of grief takes up the most room in this second poem. Grief is demonstrated largely through flashbacks that tell the story again but also by giving way to waves of emotion that the flashbacks stir up. These two ways of bringing to the surface the pain deep in the community's hearts weave a pattern of articulated grief that runs through the poem and splits it into two blocks, stanzas 1–10 and 11–22. In the first block, there are three movements from factual aspects of the past crisis to consequent feelings of distress. The first movement covers stanzas 1–5 and portrays the objective crisis up to the second line of stanza 5 before turning to a response of moaning in the third line. The second movement runs from stanza 6 to the first line of stanza 9, telling what happened, and devotes the two closing lines to a metaphorical display of grief. The third movement starts in the second line of stanza 9 and continues to the end of stanza 10, giving that stanza over to sorrow after earlier factual narration. So there is a rhythm, an initial portrayal of objective crisis and its perpetuation in emotional distress. The only exception to this structuring is the grieving exclamation *How terrible that . . . !* that opens the poem, as it did the former one.

In the second block of this second poem, the alternating rhythm is reversed in two movements, in stanzas 11–17 and 18–22. Distress is given a prior place in the first two lines of stanza 11 and in stanzas 18 and 19, and it is explained in concrete terms from the third line of stanza 11 to stanza 17 and in stanzas 20–22.

The word *ground* recurs (Gous 1993, 356–57), functioning as an artistic device that binds together facts and the feelings they generated. It is a place associated in stanzas 1, 2, and 21 with degrading facts that made the community hit bottom and in stanzas 9–11 with downcast feelings of sorrow. The word appears at strategic points, at the beginning and end of each of the two blocks. Its pervasiveness attests the merging of external experience and internal pain, so that the community not only had landed in the dirt but also was kept there in its continuing grief.

The second poem, like the first, takes the form of an alphabetic acrostic, with each of the twenty-two stanzas beginning with the successive letter of the Hebrew alphabet. The poem in its original language loudly ticks its way all round the clock, as it were, recording the relentless pace of perpetual grief. Then the grief will continue into the third and fourth alphabetic poems, like a stopwatch reset and reset again.

The second poem has a narrower focus than does the first one in that it particularly echoes the second half of the first poem. There the interpretation of the crisis drew on two prophetic traditions, the day of the Lord, which it used as a literary frame, and God's providential intervention in Judah's world. Here too the day of the Lord is a frame, now for the whole poem, occurring in the first stanza (*his day of anger*) and the last two (*your day of anger, Yahweh's day of anger*). But in this case the day carries only a past, sinister aspect and not the relatively reassuring future one that closed the previous poem. This poem also brings to the fore Yahweh's fateful intervention in stanzas 1–8, where the reporter picks up and endorses Zion's first outburst in stanzas 12–15 of the first poem. These two negative prophetic elements continue into the second poem and intensify their message of the serious spiritual trouble in which Judah had landed, from which appeal to Yahweh was the only hope of extricating itself. The congregation had to come to terms with their tragic past, taking responsibility for it and making fresh contact with God. These were the only paths toward any kind of resolution.

God's Awesome Anger at Work (2:1–5)

The first five stanzas, which move from past suffering to the grieving worry it caused, are a large enough slice for readers to digest.

¹How terrible that the Lord in his anger is
        beclouding
    Lady Zion
by having thrown down from sky to ground
    Israel's glory
and given his footstool no thought
    on his day of anger!

²The Lord destroyed with no mercy
    all of Jacob's pastures.
He tore down in his wrath
    Lady Judah's fortresses.
He brought to the ground in dishonor
    the realm and its royal officials.

³He hacked off in burning anger
    every horn Israel had.
He held back their right hands
    when the enemy appeared
and set Jacob ablaze with flaming fire, as it were,
    which spread as it consumed.

⁴Stringing his bow like an enemy,
    he stood with his right hand ready.
Just like a foe he killed
    all those regarded of high value.
Lady Zion's tent he overwhelmed
    with the fire of his fury, as it were.

⁵The Lord took on an enemy's role,
    destroying Israel
by destroying all of Zion's fortified buildings
    and wrecking Israel's fortresses,
and bringing to Lady Judah
    so much moaning and groaning.

Why is such strong language used of God? Because it reflects
the warfare erupting in Judah's backyard, of bombs, as it were,
falling on the fields of Judah's farms and in the streets of Judah's
towns—and a basic, awesome claim that Judah's own God was

paradoxically and providentially behind the firestorm. That had been the earlier claim in advance by Judah's prophets, to which this vehement way of speaking is a solemn amen. In Isaiah's classic terms, spoken in Yahweh's name, the Assyrian enemy in an earlier decade was "the rod of my anger": "I dispatch him against a people who anger me, to seize loot and snatch plunder, and to trample them down like mud in the streets" (Isa. 10:5–6). And that people was Judah. The preexilic prophets habitually made such claims. Lamentations turns them into postmortem reports that verify the prophets' prognosis. The brutal warfare of the seventh and sixth centuries BCE was for the canonical prophets and Lamentations alike the outworking of the divine will. "What will you do on the day of reckoning," asked Isaiah again, "when disaster comes from afar? . . . Nothing will remain but to cringe among the captives or fall among the slain" (Isa. 10:3–4). So this poem makes use of a series of vehement metaphors to reinforce that claim, taking its cue from the prophets as grim preachers of gospel truth, of brimstone and hellfire translated into the reality of military invasion. The human *enemy* makes fleeting appearances, in stanzas 3, 7, and 22 as the pawn of a divine opponent. The imagery is an endeavor to convey Yahweh's "strange work" and "alien task" (Isa. 28:21) and so to portray this other face of Israel's God. What might otherwise be read as accusations of God are tributes to the exercise of divine justice. This severe material is meant to be read against the backdrop of preexilic prophetic literature, as an endorsement of its claims.

The section before us, in its depiction of misery and preoccupation with the past, has the tone of a funeral dirge, which will continue until the end of stanza 17. As in the first poem, most of the lines have the limping meter of the dirge in the Hebrew. Unlike a real dirge, Yahweh is not only acknowledged but also plays a key role. However, the element of contrast characteristic of the dirge occurs in the first stanza, along with the dirgelike exclamation, the initial shriek repeated from the start of the previous poem. This shriek, whether voiced aloud or in the soul, is the alarm signal of grief, like a smoke alarm reacting to a fire. Joyce Brothers calls grief itself "one long wail of despair" (1990, 8). In a similar vein, Gerald Sittser calls an early chapter in his book "The Silent Scream of Pain" and closes it in this way: "The accident set off a silent scream of pain within my soul. That scream was so loud that I could hardly hear another sound, not for a long time, and could not imagine that I would hear any sound but that scream of pain for the rest of my life" (1996, 54). Here such a scream is articulated and broken into terrible detail.

The flashback is an interpretive one that develops the latter half of the first poem. In this second poem, the prophetic motifs of the day of the Lord and of God's destructive intervention are reiterated. Once more prophetic traditions stand in the background, as eventually stanza 17 will state plainly. Yahweh's grim future for Israel in the prophetic literature has now been transmuted into cold fact. The verb *destroy* with its divine subject and past reference becomes a keyword of stanzas 1–8, occurring four times. And Berlin draws attention to the uncompromising negativity conveyed in stanzas 1, 2, and 8, a negativity that will be perpetuated in stanzas 14, 17, 21, and 22.

Another glance over this first section shows that it refers to Zion and to Israel/Jacob/Judah, to the overthrow of their solid structures and solemn institutions. Capital and nation were joint victims of God's anger. In the Prophets, divine anger is associated particularly with the day of the Lord, as in stanza 12 of the first poem, and generally with coming divine intervention. So its appearance here is appropriate. But its frequency takes the reader's breath away: *anger*, *wrath*, and *fury* permeate the stanzas. *Fire* is used as its metaphorical and partly literal weapon of destruction, as in stanza 13 of the first poem. Explicit mention of Israel's wrongdoing is rare in the second poem, appearing only in stanza 14, while it is implied in stanza 8. A focus on anger takes its place. Anger was a feature of the day of the Lord in the first poem (stanza 12). While this association continues in the second, anger is also used more generally. In the Old Testament, anger is by no means a permanent attribute of God but an event-oriented term that describes an intermittent reaction, as Westermann has rightly observed. The reaction is to human wrongdoing. This is what *anger* reflects here, presupposing the prophets' constant reasoning that God's people had gone off the moral and spiritual rails.

Sometimes, it is true, especially in the Psalms, God's anger is perceived as an amoral force that is regarded as the mysterious source of a particular crisis. A moral ingredient is essentially missing from this usage, and the clue is an absence of reference to human sinning from the context. Psalm 102:10 is one example, in contrast to Psalm 38:1–5. If Lamentations 2 is meant to be read after the first poem, there can be no doubt that a moral cause underlies this demonstration of divine anger, and indeed stanza 14 in the present poem will refer explicitly to Zion's *wrongdoing*. Moreover, there is a telling parallel in the third poem, at lines 42–45. There a brief description of the community's suffering at the hands of an angry God is prefaced with the language of repentance in line 41 because such divine intervention is meant as a response to the community's sinning.

The preponderance of *Lord* for Yahweh in this section can be explained as a counterpart to Israel's repudiation of Yahweh's lordship, as in the first poem. According to the prophets, a whole history of deterioration had to be countered. "This history with its own irresistible and irreversible momentum . . . requires drastic measures; it must be brought to an end" (Patrick 1981, 87). That end is memorialized here.

The first stanza bemoans Zion's fall from grace. It hails Zion as formerly *Israel's glory*, employing a term used like this about another city in Isaiah 13:19, and as Yahweh's *footstool*, a place where God had been vitally present in blessing, a larger counterpart of the ark in the temple (Pham 1999, 119; Frevel 2002, 104–11). But now these lofty roles were true only of a bygone past. The divine presence had since been manifested negatively in a lingering storm cloud of retribution. The remaining four stanzas of the section first elaborate this awesome destruction in terms of the nation (stanza 2 to the second line of stanza 4) and then include the capital's fate in the final part of the section. Solid structures, as much icons of stability as were the World Trade Center towers, had been demolished. Who did this? The invading troops who had swept across the country and victoriously reached Jerusalem as their Berlin? That is only a partial answer. For the most part they are blatantly replaced by Yahweh, whose instruments the troops were deemed to be, just as Assyria was "the rod of" Yahweh's "anger" against Judah in Isaiah 10:5. Confronted by such a coalition of enemies, Judah's military forces stood no chance.

Why does Israel have horns? This imagery derives from wild oxen, whose horns symbolized their strength and were tossed in the air to celebrate a successful fight, as stanza 17 will portray. Judah's martial horns were metaphorically cut off, rendering its troops powerless. Judah was left to moan, initiating the intense grief the listening congregation still felt. The grief story has been told once more, reinforcing Zion's version in the first poem as a military calamity that was also a confrontation with an angry God. The people's underlying accountability, to which Yahweh reacted, had to be taken seriously.

God's Systematic Destruction of Zion (2:6–10)

The next two sections that move from disaster to distress in the course of stanzas 6–10 may be taken together. They focus on the fate of Jerusalem. *Indignant anger*, which does not simply act but reacts to something terribly wrong, has a single mention at the outset, but there can be no doubt that its force extends throughout.

71

⁶Moreover, he violently attacked his tabernacle as if
    a garden hut,
      wrecking his meeting place.
Yahweh turned into memories
      Zion's festivals and Sabbaths
and scorned in his indignant anger
      the king and priests.

⁷The Lord repudiated his own altar,
      spurned his sanctuary.
He delivered into the enemy's hands
      the walls of Zion's fortified buildings.
The clamor they made in Yahweh's temple
      was as loud as at festival time.

⁸It was Yahweh's plan to wreck
      Lady Zion's wall.
Having stretched out the line, he permitted his hand
      no restraint from destroying it.
So he brought mourning to rampart and wall;
      they both keeled over.

⁹Her gates sank down into the ground
      after he had shattered and ruined her bars.
Her king and royal officials went to be among other
      nations.
There was no priestly instruction,
while her prophets found
      no revelation from Yahweh.

¹⁰Sitting on the ground in silence
      are Lady Zion's old men
after throwing dirt on their heads
      and donning sackcloth.
Jerusalem's girls have bowed
      their heads to the ground.

In Judah's war, even the temple, which was so closely associated with Yahweh (*his*), had been the object of attack, so that a whole religious way of life had been swept away. The privileged roles of

72

priests and the king, who had special functions in temple worship (cf. 2 Kings 23:1–3), now evidently meant nothing to Yahweh, who scrapped them. In the course of the telling of the destruction of temple and city, a note of cruel irony is struck. The raucous noise the ravaging troops made in the temple area (cf. Ps. 74:4) had been eerily reminiscent of the noisy worship of pilgrim crowds at festival time. The contrast specifies a poignant reversal the war had caused. William C. Dix's hymn "Alleluia, Sing to Jesus" has a line relevant for the simile: "Hark! The songs of peaceful Zion thunder like a mighty flood."

As this installment of the story draws to a close, there is a brief reflection on Yahweh's purposefulness in destroying the city wall. It will be elaborated later in stanza 17. A prophetic metaphor that illustrates the execution of this purposefulness is then used; Isaiah 34:11 and 2 Kings 21:13 may be compared. The metaphor envisions Yahweh as a demolition worker who comes to a building already condemned as unfit for habitation, marks out what is to be destroyed, and then demolishes it (Dobbs-Allsopp 2004, 46n79). Jerusalem had been found seriously wanting, it is implied. The metaphor of executed judgment, like that of the divine anger, alludes to the real cause of Jerusalem's destruction. The city wall and gates are figuratively portrayed as collapsing in grief, overwhelmed by their inability to protect the capital any more. Her gates went into mourning, as in Isaiah 3:26 and Jeremiah 14:2. Destruction and distress are fused together, so that the story of one embraces the other.

The third movement from calamity to sorrow is brief. Still in prophetic mode, it switches from divine intervention to its human consequences, as Zion did in her second outburst in the first poem. Jerusalem suffered the loss of long-established authority figures, civil and religious. The royal court was deported, and the religious institutions of priesthood and prophecy collapsed. The response of sorrow is now given more space than the calamity that caused it. Among those who were left, the tragedy created an uncommon harmony for spectrums of age and gender. The citizens, as one, gave way to grief. The old engaged in traditional mourning rites, while the young, less versed in these rites, grieved in their own way, suspending their usual animation and engagement with life. The keyword of the poem, *ground*, strikingly occurs twice in the tenth stanza, underlining the intensity of the people's grief.

A Sea of Troubles (2:11–17)

[11]I am crying my eyes out.
   It has become a gut-wrenching experience for
      me.
My bile is spilled on the ground
   over "my poor people's catastrophe,"
when young children and babies collapsed
   in the town squares,

[12](when) they kept asking their mothers,
   "Where is grain and wine?"
as they collapsed, as if wounded soldiers,
   in the city squares,
their lives ebbing away
   in their mothers' arms.

[13]What analogy, what comparison with you can I
      make,
   Lady Jerusalem?
What parallel with you can I draw to comfort you,
   young Lady Zion?
Your catastrophe was so vast, like the ocean:
   who can cure you of it?

[14]The revelations your prophets had provided for you
      were empty and bland,
exposing no wrongdoing of yours
   so your fortunes could be restored.
Instead, what they provided for you
   were empty and misleading oracles.

¹⁵Passersby all clap their hands
    at you in derision.
They whistle and shake their heads
    at Lady Jerusalem (asking),
"Is this the city once called
    'perfectly beautiful,'
    'appreciated worldwide'?"

¹⁶Staring at you openmouthed
    were all your enemies.
Whistling and gnashing their teeth,
    they said, "We have destroyed her.
At last this is the day we've been patiently waiting
    for.
We are experiencing it, we can see it."

¹⁷Yahweh did what he had purposed;
    he executed his threat,
the orders he had given over a long period of time.
He tore down with no mercy,
    enabling the enemy to laugh at you
    and your foes to raise their horns high.

The reporter had given vent to his personal grief in the initial scream (stanza 1), which repeated the opening of the first poem. Otherwise he has limited himself thus far to exclamations of sorrow that acknowledge the community's grief. Now he strikingly goes much further, with a visceral outburst of his own, like Zion's in stanza 20 of the first poem. "Grief comes in waves, paroxysms, sudden apprehensions that weaken the knees and blind the eyes and obliterate the dailiness of life" (Didion 2006, 27). A psychotherapist who worked on the sixty-second floor of the World Trade Center and underwent the trauma of 9/11 later found herself counseling other survivors, like the reporter in our text. Her experience was like his: "As I constantly straddled the line between helper and survivor, an insidious toll began to be exacted. I noticed that the line between helper and trauma survivor was being blurred and difficult to maintain" (Daniels 2004, 116).

My poor people's catastrophe appears to be a quotation from Jeremiah 8:21, where all the Hebrew terms are the same (NRSV, "my poor people's hurt"). There the grief was Jeremiah's, as he looked ahead with foreboding to the tragedy of 586 BCE. His grief was a measure of the grim extent of the disaster. So it is here, but the reporter takes over the prophet's language to define the now-realized tragedy, to which he reacts with psychosomatic dimensions of sorrow. As Ann Weems testifies in two of her lament psalms, "We are the ones / who cry in the night, / the ones whose hearts pound, / whose stomachs knot, / whose heads split in pain," and "My blood pressure climbs, / and I have aches / and pains / that have no cause except / my broken heart" (1995, 84, 86).

Catastrophe occurs in both the eleventh and thirteenth stanzas, and the material in between is meant as a case study illustrating its dire degree. The death of starving children during the siege of Jerusalem is cited, while the anguish of *their* helpless *mothers* is poignantly evoked in the repetition that forms a frame for stanza 12. The death of *wounded soldiers* during wartime is something one can regrettably get used to and even hail as heroic, but the collateral dying of children is much harder to bear. The reporter, turning to address Zion, endorses her unique perception of her grief that she expressed in stanza 12 of the first poem. Such poignant suffering must generate inconsolable grief, he says. Words fail him. He has been emotively building up to this address by describing a nadir of suffering, and the congregation is meant to let it all tug at their own heartstrings and let it stimulate an expression of their own grief.

Comparing the catastrophe to the ocean illustrates its overwhelming extent, the totality of its suffering, like Hamlet's "sea of troubles." The ocean "stretches infinitely, wildly, and with no limits in sight" (O'Connor 2002, 38). One also needs to appreciate that in the Bible the sea is a symbol of chaos and negativity, which is why removal of the sea in Revelation 21:1 is a promise of blessing. The catastrophe is said to be virtually incurable—the

Hebrew word for *catastrophe* also means "wound," as the NIV renders it. The wounds of war were still festering in the people's souls. Could anyone heal them? No, unless perhaps Yahweh might be brought into the situation by way of appeal. There is an implicit reference to a heavenly helper (Kaiser). In the next section, beyond stanza 17, this possibility will be implicitly aired. The rhetorical question is broached here in the hope that it will cease to be merely rhetorical.

Stanzas 15–17 explain the vastness of the catastrophe by probing its network of causes and consequences through the different eyes of, first, passersby, then the invading enemy, and finally Yahweh. But the fourteenth stanza pauses to reflect on those causes of the catastrophe that lay behind the divine intervention. Although the primary cause was Zion's *wrongdoing*, there was an intermediate cause, the prewar messages of Zion's *prophets*. Rudolph defines *your prophets* as the wrong type of prophets preferred by Zion. In the prophetic books "the prophets," confusingly perhaps, can refer, as here, to a stream of prophetic tradition alien to that of the canonical prophets. The latter tradition is summarized in Jeremiah 28:8 and is contrasted with oracles of peace in 28:9. Jeremiah 23:9–40 is a collection of messages against "the prophets," while 23:22 mentions their failure to turn the people from their "evil ways," lulling the people into unrealistic complacency rather than counseling repentance. Their positive messages had no room for negative analysis. So these prophets, ignoring the people's culpability, had not served them well.

Stanzas 15 and 16 revert to the divinely caused catastrophe but in particular narrate its humiliating human consequences. The fifteenth stanza, recalling the passersby mentioned in the first poem (stanza 12) and using the standard language found in 1 Kings 9:8, describes their reaction to Zion's catastrophe, their mixed feelings of shock and contempt at Jerusalem's ruined state. Clapping hands seem here to be a gesture of ridicule, as in Job 27:23. There is a dirgelike contrast to the city's past glory, which draws on the Zion tradition as it finds literary expression first in Psalm 50:2 and then in Psalm 48:2 (literally, "the joy of all the earth"). Other negative feelings—negative for Zion—had been expressed earlier in time by the invaders. They had crowed over the collapse of Jerusalem, celebrating it as a strategic objective come true after a long military campaign. Gnashing teeth is a gesture of mockery, as in Psalm 35:16. *Destroyed* echoes God's own work in stanzas 2, 5, and 8. Unwittingly, these human enemies were divine agents. Moreover, their awaited *day* was really a manifestation of Yahweh's day. "Zion's enemies are but the players on the stage. It is God who directs the action" (Provan 1991, 75).

In fact, stanza 17 stands in pointed contrast to the limited viewpoint of the victors (Gottlieb 1978, 35; Renkema). Rudolph has called this stanza "the quintessence of the whole chapter" (1962, 225). It reverts to the underlying factor of Yahweh's intervention and hails it as the fulfillment of the true, long-standing prophetic tradition. The divine orders have the same prophetic sense as in stanza 17 of the first poem. Jeremiah 28:8 expresses this tradition as the divine use of "war, disaster, and plague" announced "from early times." Yahweh's mercilessness, already mentioned in the second stanza, was part of the future judgment predicted by pre-586 BCE prophets: Isaiah (Isa. 30:14 NJB), Jeremiah (Jer. 13:14), and especially Ezekiel (for example, Ezek. 5:11). It is an aspect of the totality of suffering Judah was to experience in retribution for its wrongdoing, and one that Lamentations claims it did experience. This divine mystery had to be factored into the understanding of Zion and so of the grieving congregation. The catastrophe was essentially a spiritual matter between Zion and her God. As Zechariah later reported, "Did not my words and my decrees, which I commanded my servants the prophets, overtake your forefathers?" (Zech. 1:6). This nettle had to be firmly grasped in order that their grief could be properly worked through.

A Call to Zion to Pray and Zion's Prayer (2:18–22)

In stanzas 18 and 19 the reporter urges prayer, and in stanzas 20–22 Zion takes his advice.

> [18]Call out to the Lord,
> > you wall of Lady Zion.
> Let your tears run down like a torrent
> > day and night.
> Grant yourself no respite,
> > the pupils of your eyes no pause.
>
> [19]Get up, shout out during the night,
> > from the start of the night watches.
> Pour out in a flood what is on your heart
> > in the presence of the Lord himself.
> Raise your hands to him
> > over the lost lives of your little children,
> who collapsed from hunger
> > at every street corner.
>
> [20]"Look, Yahweh, and take notice.
> > On whom else have you ever inflicted this—
> when women were 'eating the fruit of their wombs,'
> > the little children they had held in their arms,
> when priests and prophets were being killed
> > in the Lord's sanctuary,
>
> [21](when) lying on the ground in the streets
> > were males young and old,
> (when) my boys and girls fell,
> > victims of the sword—
> you killed them on your day of anger,
> > slaughtering with no mercy.
>
> [22]You invited as if for festival time
> > my 'terrors from everywhere around,'
> and there was found on Yahweh's day of anger
> > no refugee, no survivor.
> As for children I had held in my arms and raised,
> > my enemy annihilated them."

The reporter's call for prayer represents a radical change from the poem's earlier tone of dirge to the prayer language of the psalm lament. This language moves beyond the dirge by bringing God into the equation as a present factor, here in order that Zion may make her confession. The surprising call to Zion's wall, rather than to Zion herself, picks up the reference to the wall in the eighth stanza, which not only identified it as both suffering from divine destruction and metaphorically engaging in grief but also linked the destruction to Yahweh's deliberate planning revealed earlier by the prophets, rather like stanza 17. That grieving over implicitly merited destruction is now to be brought to God in prayer. Zion is to grieve face-to-face with the destroying God. By this means Zion endorses the reporter's interpretation of the catastrophe, and so she is freed to move forward. *Get up* is a call for a turning point (Berges).

The call to prayer is also a call to continuing and intense grief throughout the night (cf. Ps. 63:6). Coherent words and wordless tears are to mingle, bringing to the surface the heartfelt pain left by the tragedy. A torrent of tears is to be matched by a flood of words. The reporter suggests as a prayer topic his own source of deepest grief, the deaths of children who starved during the siege, which he had narrated in detail in stanzas 11 and 12. Who could resist such an emotive call? He puts tremendous pressure on Zion and, through her, on the as yet silent congregation whom she represents.

Zion complies in stanzas 20–22. When Zion asks Yahweh to *look and take notice*, she seeks a divine acknowledgment that she has satisfied the prophetic program of destruction and extreme suffering for God's own people and has come to a corresponding self-understanding, in accord with the reporter's lead. She gives four examples of her traumatic suffering, beginning and ending her prayer with the heartbreaking issue of her dead children, who had died either of starvation during the siege or more directly at the enemies' hands after the city fell. The human consequences of the catastrophe are seen as precisely that, consequences of Yahweh's direct intervention, which the reporter had interpreted in terms of the canonical prophets' predictions. Such grim human experience and divine providence had been two sides of the same coin, just as the reporter had claimed. House observes that stanza 21 contains a remarkable concentration of previously used terms, in acceptance of what the reporter had said. Zion's prayer is another version of her admission *Yahweh is the one in the right* in stanza 18 of the first poem. This version is crafted according to the particular concerns of the second poem. There is one corroboration from Deuteronomy 28, which had featured so much in the first poem, from Deuteronomy 28:53 (also compare in general Jer. 19:9). That dire forecast had come tragically true. Zion had been singled out for its fulfillment. Out of desperation, bodies of the children who had died of starvation had been gruesomely used as food by the survivors, including their mothers. Elaboration of this once unimaginable horror will be given in stanza 10 of the fourth poem. The ghastly memory triggers other shocking memories relating to the aftermath of the siege, as the invaders rushed in—the killing of religious personnel in the temple grounds and the general massacre of old and young in the streets.

All this was the consequence of divine intervention, so divine and human hostilities are interwoven in the prayer. The prophetic motif of the day of the Lord is mentioned twice in order to reinforce the note of fulfillment. And it is twice associated with *anger*, the reporter's earlier means of expressing Yahweh's inevitable reaction to all that had gone terribly wrong in Judah. For good measure, there is an echo of a prophetic phrase, Jeremiah's catchphrase for the invading forces, "terror from everywhere around" (e.g., Jer. 6:25). The phrase *my terrors from everywhere around* has a parallel later in the stanza: *my enemy*, which echoes the human *enemy* of stanzas 3 and 7. The invaders were Yahweh's invited guests, the macabre counterpart of pilgrims flocking to the city of God. Zion's prayer can even endorse *with no mercy*, the prophetic motif the reporter had used earlier in stanzas 2 and 17. The totality of the killing is pardonable hyperbole. The prayer is a soulful series of amens to the reporter's prophetic interpretation of the tragedy, to which Zion's *wrongdoing* (stanza 14) had necessarily brought her. The prayer is a prayer of confession, which Zion needed to bring as her own consequence. Will the listening congregation follow her lead?

An analogous example comes from my experience as a chaplain. One patient who requested a chaplain's visit was a drunk driver. Andrew was in the rehabilitation unit, recovering from an accident he had caused, but he was unlikely to walk again. His religion was listed as "none" in his chart. It turned out that he did not want any spiritual help, just someone to talk to regularly in order to relieve the tedium of his long hospital stay. I took on that role and week by week watched him grow stronger and able to leave his bed and maneuver his new wheelchair, a masterpiece of engineering of which he became the proud captain. I wondered whether he would ever begin a sentence with "I've been thinking about my accident . . ." Andrew never did, nor did he in any other way express any regrets over his drinking and the physical handicap it had caused. In his case there was no evident grief, just silent denial, and I never found out if he planned to give up his drinking.

More usually, drunk driving leads not only to catastrophe and physical suffering but also to emotional grief and remorse. Alcoholics Anonymous is there to pick up the pieces for any drinkers prepared to give up their denial. AA has a good record of bringing alcoholics to a sense of moral responsibility as a necessary part of sobriety. The self-caused suffering of the alcoholic does have some parallels with the case with which the book of Lamentations is dealing, although the latter case is a specialized one and incapable of application in all its aspects to most who grieve. However, in some respects it overlaps with the approach of AA: alcoholics suffer the side effects of relying on alcohol. They fail to achieve the things they want to achieve and become unable to manage their lives in any number of aspects, such as Wilcox (1998, 40–43) has illustrated. The twelve-step program of recovery taught by AA addresses such problems. Accepting responsibility for one's actions is advocated by step 4: "We made a searching and fearless moral inventory of ourselves." Contact with God by means of prayer is urged in step 11: "We sought through prayer and meditation to improve our conscious contact with God as we understood Him." The ultimate goal is set out in step 2: "We came to believe that a Power higher than ourselves could restore us to sanity." The prospect of this ultimate goal has to await specific mention in the third poem of Lamentations, but accountability has been an overt and underlying theme of the first two poems, and so has turning to God in prayer. Above all, the meetings of AA provide a forum for alcoholics to tell their story again and again and encourage them to process their grief and move through it. The liturgical gatherings behind the book of Lamentations were not unlike AA meetings. The poems have demonstrated empathy with the victims and were meant to induce them to articulate their sorrow and relate to God.

3

Third Poem (Lamentations 3)

The Wounded Healer

The concept of the wounded healer comes from Greek legends about the centaur Chiron, a healer who received an incurable wound from a poisoned arrow, and about Asclepius, another healer who was wounded and killed by a thunderbolt of Zeus for taking his healing art beyond human bounds, as far as the raising of the dead. The psychologist Carl Jung used the concept with the accent on *wounded*, as a warning that the psychotherapist is in danger of being hurt by the wounds of his or her clients and needs self-care. But, speaking of this wounding of the healer by the patient, he went on to maintain that "it is his own hurt that is the measure of his power to heal" (1954, 116). Popular usage employs the concept positively, with the emphasis on healing, to indicate that personal suffering can create a deep reservoir of comfort and strength from which others may draw and find new life.

Henri Nouwen wrote a book for pastors titled *The Wounded Healer*, in which he affirmed that the pastor has the opportunity of using his or her experience of wounding to help other wounded souls, though he also warned of the risk of being wounded by so doing (1972, 72). Within each person there is woundedness and healing. When wound meets wound, sympathy results, but this is not always trustworthy. An infected wound can pour its infection into the other person. If the healer side tries to touch the other's wound with its healing, it may result in an attempt to fix the other. But when both sides are available, healer calls to healer in the other; wound identifies with wound. Empathy results, compassion connects, and hope is transmitted. "Showing others who suffer how we were given help is the very thing which makes life seem so worth while to us now," claims *The Big Book* of Alcoholics Anonymous (2001, 124), adding, "Cling to the thought that in God's hands the dark past is the greatest possession you have—the key to life and happiness to others." Small wonder AA insists that it takes an alcoholic to help an alcoholic.

If we place the concept of the wounded healer in a biblical context, we cannot fail to recall the community's grateful testimony about the Servant in Isaiah 53:5, "by his wounds we are healed," which the New Testament interprets in terms of the crucified Jesus (1 Pet. 2:24). Another parallel lies here before us, I suggest. The third poem of Lamentations exemplifies Nouwen's pastoral message. When we read lines 25–51, we recognize a preached sermon, which aims to talk helpfully about God and human suffering as described in Lamentations and then closes with a call to prayer. What makes the sermon special is its introduction (lines 1–24), which consists of a personal testimony about the preacher's suffering and the roundabout journey of faith that it started. This long and emotional testimony shows that the preacher has sat where the congregation in turn sits. His experience lends a unique validity and sensitivity to his sermon. As Weiser observes, it gives him leave to speak, since he has learned what he is now teaching others. Out of his own journey come resources the congregation may respect and warm to. "We asked our clerics if they had lost a child," wrote some bereaved parents, "feeling that unless they had experienced such a loss themselves, they could not fully understand the depths of our grief" (Barkin et al. 2004, 17). Here in turn is a preacher who has lived out the theology he teaches, one who is a battle-scarred witness to its truth. This experience lends credibility and stature to his ministry. One of the tasks of a caregiver is to "assist the griever in reestablishing a system of belief" (Rando 1984, 102), and this caregiver uses his spiritual experience to discharge that task.

A first glance at this poem in any Bible seems to indicate that it is three times as long as either of the preceding poems. However, this is a fallacy. It does have sixty-six verses, over against their twenty-two, but the change in numbering is due to a different type of alphabetic acrostic. In the previous poems, only the first line of each stanza began with a successive letter of the Hebrew alphabet. In this case, the three lines of a stanza all begin with the same letter. The numbering remains letter-sensitive, and so extra numbering has been used to correspond with the Hebrew letters, marking lines rather than the twenty-two stanzas, but in the tally of stanzas and lines this poem is no longer than the first or second poems. The more intensive acrostic form and the new way of numbering bear witness to a special role the third poem has in the book. It functions as a rhetorical climax for the first two poems. It reinforces their totality of suffering, once more using predominantly the dirge meter in the Hebrew, but it advances their position. The poem has been artistically highlighted to enhance this advance in content, which takes it substantially beyond the concerns shared by the first two.

Nevertheless, this poem has close developmental continuity with the first two, in content as well as in acrostic form. It continues the theological interpreting undertaken in the earlier poems but does so with an extra, positive emphasis. We began study of the second poem by drawing a comparison between the first two poems and Joel 1:2–2:17, observing that both passages exhibit a growing intensity of appeal. A direct call to repentance in Joel 2:12–13a is lacking in the first and second poems of Lamentations. Such a call now turns up, however, in the third poem at stanza 14 (lines 40–42). Moreover, the encouraging characterization of God as "abounding in love" in Joel 2:13b accords with mention of the Lord's *abundant grace* in stanza 11 (line 32); the Hebrew is practically the same. Last, the third poem develops and brings to an interim conclusion a process of putting increasing pressure on the listening congregation to offer their own prayers of grief to God. Stanzas 14–16 (lines 40–47) reiterate more directly the recommendations to Zion to pray that closed the former two poems.

Weiser, Davidson, Provan, Droin, and Bracke are surely right in maintaining that readers are meant to identify the speaker as the same main character who appeared hitherto in the role of reporter. Provan compares the similar personal outbursts of grief here in line 48 and in stanza 11 of the second poem, which features the same compassionate reaction. In this poem, the reporter continues the first-person language he used there in stanzas 11 and 13. After edging forward in the second poem, he now takes center stage. Instead of continuing to address Zion, he now bypasses her and turns directly to the listening congregation represented by Zion and urges them to pray. They will duly respond in the fifth poem. The third poem functions as an interim conclusion that looks ahead to the real conclusion. Prayer will be a necessary and decisive step forward in the congregation's processing of its grief.

His Testimony of Guilty Wounds (3:1–16)

Lines 1–24 belong together as a testimony to personal suffering in lines 1–16 and to a reaction to that suffering that gradually changes from pessimism to optimism in lines 17–24. In the first part of the testimony, the reporter continues his account from the first two poems but now reports his own suffering. In the translation, the numbering of the twenty-two stanzas is indicated in parentheses.

(1) ¹I am a man who once experienced affliction
     from his rod of wrath.
²I am someone he led off, bringing me
     into darkness devoid of light.
³I am someone he repeatedly
     turned his hand against, time after time.

(2) ⁴He damaged my skin and flesh,
     broke my bones.
⁵He mounted a siege all round me,
     a siege that left me bitter and worn-out.
⁶He made me stay in a dark place
     like one where people lie forever dead.

(3) ⁷He walled me in so I could not get out,
     weighed me down with chains.
⁸Though I kept on calling out, shouting for help,
     he stopped my prayer.
⁹He obstructed my path with a wall of stone blocks,
     disrupting my route.

(4) ¹⁰He assumed with me the role of a bear lying in wait,
     a lion in hiding.
¹¹Taking me off my path, he mangled me
     and left me devastated.
¹²Stringing his bow, he took aim at me,
     using me as a target for his arrow.

(5) ¹³He shot right into my kidneys
     the contents of his quiver.
¹⁴I became a laughingstock to all my people,
     ridiculed by them all the time.
¹⁵He fed me full of bitter herbs,
     gave me too much wormwood to drink.

(6) ¹⁶And he was responsible for my teeth being broken
          on gravel,
     for my being pushed down into the dirt.

89

The reporter speaks in the first person, in continuation of stanzas 11–13 in the second poem, before Zion spoke in the closing prayer. He talks about his own suffering in a derivative way, deliberately leaning back on descriptions of suffering given before. That is immediately evident from the opening phrase, *his rod of wrath*, which, as Rudolph observes, both assumes from the foregoing poem that Yahweh is meant as the agent and picks up from there the motif of anger. Also, the reporter adopts a style of speaking that readers have encountered before, first on Zion's lips in her first outburst in the initial poem (stanzas 12–15), then repeated in the reporter's speech about Zion's suffering (stanzas 1–8 of the second poem), and finally resumed in the course of Zion's prayer (stanzas 20–22). This derivative style takes over the understanding of a prophetic background, echoing the form of an announcement of disaster, which forecast the destructive intervention of Israel's God in the delinquent human scene and the grim consequences of that intervention. Not that the reporter is claiming the fulfillment of prophecy in his own life; he simply wants to compare his suffering with Zion's. "His purpose is to establish a parallel between his own fate and that of Zion and the people" (Albertz 2003, 163). He has undergone similar suffering in his experience, suffering that he interprets likewise as the providential work of God. He has had to wrestle with that experience and come to terms with it. He now gives a personal testimony in order to encourage the listening congregation to trust him as he counsels them in their suffering.

The reporter talks in an impressionistic way, ransacking the lament dictionary in the Psalms and elsewhere in order to make use of a wide range of traditional language. He presents a series of images of his suffering, managing to use even more extravagant language than that found in earlier descriptions of divine judgment—and they had been couched in strong language that armchair readers find uncomfortable. This use of language that Calvin called "harsh" and "hyperbolical" (1950, 391–92) is adopted for its shock value. The reporter speaks like the pastor preaching at his son's funeral who said, "I have been to where life hurts the worst and cuts the deepest and hits the hardest. Therefore listen to me . . ." (Edington 2006, 73).

All this is part of a rhetoric of persuasion. Earlier the rhetoric was intended to convey to the congregation the reporter's empathy with their suffering and his interpretation of it. Now it is designed to assure them of the validity of his experience as a counseling credential. I remember listening to a patient who was pouring out the troubles she had been through, which had landed her in the hospital. At one point, without thinking, I murmured "I know," registering the sympathy I felt. She stopped in midstream, suddenly angry and convinced, like Zion earlier, of the uniqueness of her intense suffering. I briefly explained that I had been through a parallel experience in that one respect. From then on there was a greater rapport between us. I became more than an impersonal sounding board, and she warmed to my presence. In the same fashion, the reporter assures the congregation that he has been through a similar time of suffering, in this case to get them to accept the benefit of his experience and move forward with him.

Overwhelming pictures are drawn that are meant to communicate some crucial concepts. First, throughout the section the grim prophetic message of divine intervention and human consequences is echoed from the reporter's experience. Second, God's intervention is repeatedly described in terms of blows instead of blessings. The first line, with its mention of the *rod*, acts as a headline, and then the blows are illustrated in terms of *hand*, attacking animals, and *arrow*. Third, the normative view of human life as a progressive journey is shockingly reversed. Line 2 announces this motif. Life, being pushed off course, develops into a standstill, illustrated with images of a *siege*, confinement, and obstruction. Fourth, emotive terms are used for the consequent suffering. This concept is introduced with *darkness* in line 2 and succeeded by descriptions of pain, bitterness, exhaustion, and devastation; it includes the secondary suffering of ridicule from other people. The section persuasively portrays suffering at God's hands from these different angles. It is meant to leave no one in the listening congregation unmoved. Ascribing this suffering to God is hard for Christians to listen to. But they should not too readily retreat from it. Sometimes the Christian enters into the dark night of the soul and is constrained to use such language. C. S. Lewis, mourning the painful and lingering death of his beloved Joy, said of God, "He hurts us beyond our worst fears and beyond all we can imagine" (1976, 31).

The first stanza introduces the suffering. Here the reporter presents himself in a new guise and gives the gist of the rest of the section. From the beginning he establishes a rapport with Zion's experiences. He is a fellow victim. As a sufferer, he offers himself as a male role model, in succession to the female modeling of Zion that gained its validity from the role of professional women mourners in Israel's culture. *Affliction* is the term he had used in the first poem at stanza 3 concerning the state's suffering, while Zion applied it to herself in stanza 9.

Moreover, *wrath* not only echoes the second poem at stanza 2 but also generally reflects that poem's preoccupation with anger as God's moral reaction to human wrongdoing. The reporter's own sinning is not directly mentioned but is deftly suggested in this way. He presents himself as not standing on a higher moral ground than Zion. He is like an alcoholic who is now recovering from bad and regrettable experiences and wants his fellow alcoholics to be in recovery too. His suffering is expressed by a conventional Old Testament term of divine retribution, a *rod*, which also appears in 2 Samuel 7:14 and, in a prophetic context, in Isaiah 10:5. He had also been brought by God into the negative place of darkness and received blow after blow. The divine *hand* that had once brought blessing (cf. Ps. 104:28) now *turned* and brought only blows. Emotive language is used in lines 3 and 4 to convey the depth and breadth of his personal suffering. As Calvin said, "Darkness signifies all sorts of adversities and the sorrow which proceeds from them" (1950, 390).

In the body of this section, the listening congregation is bombarded with a succession of negative images. Those images begin in the second stanza with physical pain, a grueling military siege, and darkness once more. This time the motif of darkness is intensified by comparing it with the underworld; his experience was deathlike, so low was the quality of his life. The third stanza commences with imprisonment and concludes with a roadblock that, as in Hosea 2:6 and Job 19:8, impedes life's journey. In the middle line a more interpersonal note is struck. His ardent praying was never heard and answered, presumably because of his unresolved sinning, as in Isaiah 1:15. The first two lines of stanza 4 develop the image of a wild animal. In the first line it is a latent danger, filling its potential victim with foreboding (Labahn 2005, 88), whereas in the second it lunges and mauls. Similarly, the next pair of lines switches to an archer who first takes deliberate aim and then shoots expertly at his human target, as in the fourth stanza of the previous poem. Line 16 echoes the secondary suffering of ridicule expressed as the community's experience in the first two poems. But it also differentiates the reporter's suffering from that collective one by means of *my people*. It shows that he is drawing on a separate, personal experience for purposes of comparison. The final image in the first line of stanza 6 evokes the losing side of close combat, being flung down violently to the ground and biting the dust.

The reporter has proved his point, that his personal suffering has been comparable to Zion's and qualifies him to engage with it. He has mainly relied on stark imagery to do so. His use and range of images have endeavored to convey the reality of an unspeakable experience.

His Second Thoughts (3:17–24)

If in his earlier description of suffering the reporter made room for the emotional feelings it brought, now he turns in his testimony to the ways he thought about his suffering. This section is full of references to thinking. He confesses to a series of negative ruminations at first, but eventually reassessment led him to positive and remedial conclusions.

> ¹⁷And my mind had no room for peace;
>   I forgot what good fortune was.
> ¹⁸And I thought, "Gone is my life expectancy
>   and what I hopefully waited for from Yahweh."
>
> (7) ¹⁹Pondering my affliction and wandering
>   was tantamount to drinking bitter wormwood.
> ²⁰My mind pondered and pondered it
>   and became downcast.
> ²¹(But) this is what I recollected,
>   waiting hopefully as a consequence,
>
> (8) ²²that Yahweh's gracious acts have not ended,
>   that his compassion has not stopped.
> ²³They are renewed every morning—
>   so great is your faithfulness!
> ²⁴"Yahweh is my allocation," I thought to myself,
>   waiting hopefully for him as a consequence.

When in the previous poems the reporter had told Zion's story and let Zion tell the story for herself, that series of grim flashbacks was not lacking in theological reflection. In telling his personal story, the reporter included such reflection in his providential interpretation. But now he challenges its utter negativity by reassessing his thinking about his own pain. The point at which he challenges it is the pessimistic despair with which any victim of raw grief can identify. The accent in the stories told hitherto had been on the burden of loss and destruction. It had filled the horizon of these sufferers—the vast, chaotic ocean of grief mentioned in the second poem. The dirge-inspired poems had been preoccupied with death and deathlike experiences. The reporter had likewise portrayed his own suffering as a sort of death in the second stanza—"a semblance of living. No, not living, existing" (Brooks 1985, 16).

Now he rethinks his suffering—he does not yet venture to preach about his companions' suffering—and testifies to an astonishing change of mind. He invites them to listen to his testimony. He will describe a reflective journey that led to the development of his earlier thinking in a new and positive direction. They can reject it or accept it for themselves, but they cannot deny his conviction of its validity in his own case. At least it will open their minds to theoretical possibilities, which may lead to a crack in their mono-lithic mind-set. He hopes for the reaction of new attendees at a support group for bereaved parents: "Here were people who were living out our very own nightmare and somehow, remarkably, they were surviving" (Barkin et al. 2004, 31). What he had done, they can endeavor to do. "It is not the *experience* of loss that becomes the defining moment of our lives. . . . It is how we *respond* to loss that matters" (Sittser 1996, 9).

In the rest of the sixth stanza, the reflective journey starts from a place parallel to where the congregation is situated. *Peace* (*shalom*) and *good fortune* were conspicuous by their absence from his life. Preoccupied with the pressures of suffering, he could only meditate in a dismissive way on prospects for his future. "Discovering and mourning the lost future stories is as important as remembering and rehearsing the past stories that were meaningful" (Lester 1995, 51). For the reporter, those future stories depended on God's blessing, which then seemed a very doubtful scenario. Hope was no longer in his vocabulary. Once it had been—a strong sense of spiritual hope, rooted in Yahweh as a positive agent in his life. Re'emi observes that this is the first time in the third poem that the divine name has been used. I think this is because it is deliberately associated with a positive sentiment, even if one that is outdated at the moment. That was yesteryear's happy testimony, but a frowning providence had taught him otherwise. A chorus of amens from the congregation must have echoed his words. The reporter stays in tune with their negativity, repeating *affliction* from the first stanza, the term that united his personal suffering with that of the congregation. He also repeats *wandering*, which he had used of Jerusalem in stanza 7 of the first poem. He picks up the emotional motif of bitterness that he used earlier of himself and that had been Zion's reported experience in stanza 4 of the first poem. At this stage, his mind was as depressively made up as the congregation's minds are now. There is a short step from grief over a disruptive event to despair caused by the loss of continuity.

Suddenly, however, he reports a change of mind, as the psalmist does in Psalm 73:16–17, and switches to a new conviction of hope. It is a turning point for him, a surprising reaffirmation of what he rejected for himself at the end of the previous stanza. What can this newfound conviction be? The eighth stanza will explain. There has been a careful buildup to this transition. The initial assurance that in his totally negative attitude toward his suffering he had been of one mind with his companions made it likely that they would be prepared to hear him out, as he becomes "a witness to God's mercy before a mourning congregation" (Re'emi 1984, 102). The reporter has the audacity to return to his previous positive conception of Yahweh—he reuses the name from line 18. How can this be? He claims to find evidence of divine grace and compassion even in the midst of his experience of suffering. He discerns repeated evidence of it "every morning." As Provan comments, he has at least survived, along with the suffering people he addresses.

Survival is something to celebrate! He feels blessed just to be alive. *Still alive* in line 39 will clarify that the reference here is to survival. Sometimes survivor guilt is experienced because someone has survived and others died. In this case, that is no temptation because in the testimony no one else has been involved in the suffering, but the reporter does want the congregation to follow his example. Survival is accepted as a blessing to be appreciated. "Thank God I'm alive" is his sentiment. The antidote to despair is to "look for the signs of providence within the everyday happenings of our lives. These blessings can be found even in the midst of the traumas and tragedies that tempt us to despair" (Lester 1995, 88).

I recall a series of visits I once made to the critical care section of the neonatal unit at the hospital. In keeping with the parents' wishes, I was visiting a premature baby and praying aloud beside his crib. He looked a pitiable sight, depending on a respirator to compensate for his underdeveloped lungs, a picture of ill health. His nurse never seemed to be around to ask about little John's progress or lack of it. One day I did find her tending him and was able to ask. She had nothing to say at first and then simply said, "Where there's life, there's hope." Not much of an answer, I thought at the time. But afterwards I incorporated it into my prayers at the baby's side as something to cling to.

The reporter says, not yet about the congregation but about himself, "Where there is life, there is hope, and so amid my suffering, as long as I have life, I can also justify my hope in God." He makes a spiritual identification of that modicum of life with a positive work of God, which marks a turning point in his testimony. Earlier he disdained his meager measure of life, equating it in the second stanza with the bare existence credited to those who lie in the dark underworld. With a life like that, who needed death to come? Second thoughts prevail, however: "perhaps the present is other than the nothingness it has seemed to be. It may be that the present contains the secret of the renewal of life we long for" (Sittser 1996, 65). For the reporter, his life of sorts is like a tiny seedling, which despite being buffeted by the cruel elements is surviving and possesses the potential of growing into a beautiful, productive plant. This little life is not an end but a beginning or, better, a continuation that is renewed each morning. It is evidence, small but real, of continuing divine grace and compassion, since God is the giver and maintainer of life.

Grace translates the term in the Old Testament traditionally rendered "loving kindness" by the KJV and revised to "steadfast love" in the NRSV and "love" in the NIV. It is usually a reference to Yahweh's love for Israel, the people of the covenant. A key text is Exodus 34:6, where Yahweh is defined as "the compassionate . . . God, . . . abounding in love [or grace] and faithfulness." In the later hymns in the book of Psalms, the term is extended to the work of the creator God in maintaining the created world: "The LORD is gracious and compassionate . . . good to all; he has compassion on all he has made" (Ps. 145:8–9). Jonah fuses the two conceptions in applying Exodus 34:6 to the people of Nineveh, as he grumbles about God's sparing them (Jon. 4:2). Here in Lamentations there is a different kind of fusion. The covenant people are also creatures who enjoy God's common grace, the blessing of life. Even in their attenuated state, it is still possible to see the gracious hand of God in the fact that they have all woken up that morning. But the reporter does not venture that far. For now he only affirms it as a sustaining truth he has regained for himself in the context of his own suffering as a member of God's people. He is a survivor—thanks be to God!

A few other Old Testament texts relate God's grace to the preservation of life: Genesis 19:18–20; Psalm 119:159; and indeed Jonah 4:2 in the light of Jonah 4:11. When the Hebrew term is used of human relationships, it also has this application a number of times, such as in Genesis 20:11–13; Joshua 2:12–14; and Judges 1:24–25 (Clark 1993, 186, 262). In more general terms, one may also compare the portrayal of escaping with one's life as a divine blessing (Jer. 39:19; 45:5) and the way that surviving a God-sent calamity is likened to "a burning branch snatched from the fire" (Amos 4:11).

The reporter has managed to interpret his experience in terms of theology and to break through to a sustaining factor in a wretched life. His spiritual insight is shown in that he can see a life that to others looks like a glass nearly empty as one that has something left in it. As Paul said of himself in 2 Corinthians 4:9, "Though badly hurt . . . we are not destroyed." It is this insight that the reporter wants his listeners to realize for themselves and act on. While the suffering continued, he reached a turning point (Albertz 2003, 170), a paradigm shift he covets for the listening congregation. What Gerstenberger says of the whole poem is especially true of this part: "It is the gospel of survival that is preached here" (2001, 497).

The reporter's realization has brought some positive meaning back into his life. He has exercised "the last of the human freedoms—to choose one's attitude in any given set of circumstances." This was a truth tested out in four concentration camps by Viktor Frankl (1963, 104). And what should this attitude be? John Claypool realized after the death of his ten-year-old daughter, Laura Lue, from leukemia that "there are times . . . [when] the help God offers us is . . . to endure what cannot be changed, to allow the change to take place within us and our attitude, rather than in the outward circumstances that we face" and so "to grow on the inside rather than to change on the outside" (2006, 45–46). As a result he was able to "take every day as the gift that it is," comparing Paul's testimony to God's grace given in weakness (2 Cor. 12:9) and commenting that "sometimes the only form grace takes is the grace simply to hang in there and not give up—even that is a grace to help in time of need" (49–50). It is this sustaining grace the reporter testifies about. His testimony is that of Gerald Sittser: "I did not go through pain and come out the other side; instead I lived in it and found within that pain the grace to survive and eventually grow" (1996, 37).

Where grace appears in Old Testament texts, *compassion* often does not lag far behind, as the texts cited above demonstrate. Divine compassion is grace turned toward the human sufferer. It is a fatherly word, as Psalm 103:13 affirms and as the parable of the prodigal son reaffirms: The father, "filled with compassion, . . . ran to his son, threw his arms around him and kissed him" (Luke 15:20). The term is applied to the preservation of life in Psalm 119:77, 156 and Jonah 3:9–10. The reporter's continuing lease on life was proof to him that Yahweh was meeting at least some of his needs, which suggested that his own survival had some purpose. There is enormous theological tension in this testimony. How can God be both foe and friend? How can anger and grace coexist? Nevertheless, it is a tension the reporter insists on maintaining as he endeavors to square the complexity of experience and faith in God.

The reporter suddenly veers from talking about God to talking to God. He has done this before, in the first poem at stanza 10. In each case it is a sign of strong emotion, as when a child is suddenly moved to clutch the hand of a trusted grown-up. There it was shocked anguish—"No!"—that motivated the change. Here it is praise that breaks through the theological statements with an exclamatory "Yes!" *So great is* your *faithfulness!* A similar change occurs in the course of Psalm 23. God is spoken about in the third person until verse 4. Then a worst-case scenario prompts the psalmist to say, "You are with me," as if taking hold of God's hand for reassurance.

Divine faithfulness is the third of a trilogy of theological terms in this stanza. It occurs together with grace and compassion in Psalm 145:8, 13, while in Exodus 34:6 another form of the same Hebrew term is used. It is a word survivors can hold on to. Once again it is an extrapolation from the flickering but real embers of life the reporter still possessed. The embers were evidence of continuing positive contact with the God of life, even as suffering continued. It is unfortunate that the popular hymn based on this text, "Great Is Thy Faithfulness," detaches it from its context of brave endurance in the face of suffering, a human context inspired by divine faithfulness.

Traditional theological affirmations have surprisingly turned up in this eighth stanza in the form of key Old Testament words. The reporter has been reminding the congregation of their long-established religious faith by suggestively finding it valid for his own understanding. A final affirmation is added, this time a traditional statement. It is a spiritual metaphor that the book of Psalms delights to use. Its origin lies in the allocation of land to the tribes of Israel. Only the tribe of Levi, made up of priests and Levites, was excepted from the distribution of agricultural land to provide a living. Instead, Yahweh made provision for them: they were to live on the contributions of tithing, firstfruits, and so on, which the Israelites brought to God at the sanctuary. These contributions were passed on to the tribe dedicated to sacred service. In other words, Yahweh was their allocation, their ground of support, their livelihood (Num. 18:20, 24). Believers took up this striking truth as a metaphor to describe their own relationship to God. With second naïveté they rationalized that behind the work they did on the farm or in the potter's shop lay God's throbbing gifts of resources and energy to work and engage in all the other transactions that make up human life. Renkema observes that the Hebrew name Hilkiah, a lay as well as priestly name, reflects this spiritual truth, which parents wished their child to appreciate. It means "Yahweh is my allocation."

In the psalms, the spiritual metaphor is applied to all the different seasons of life. When life was stable, the metaphor was a confident affirmation of trust (Ps. 16:5). When life had recovered from crisis, it was claimed to be true once more (Ps. 73:26). Remarkably, when life was in doubt and crisis prevailed, it was still defiantly shouted out against the odds (Pss. 119:57; 142:5). Here there is the same defiance of circumstances. The feeble life of one who survives in the midst of death is gratefully credited to God. And this spiritual attribution gives birth to renewed hope.

101

The affirmations of stanza 8 are framed with a repeated logical conclusion, *waiting hopefully as a consequence.* The conclusions are not quite the same. In the second case it becomes more relational and derives strength from appreciating that relationship with God: *waiting hopefully for him.* True, there is a natural irksomeness about waiting, but the reporter was able to transcend it. One expects to be on the move, making progress, and that is what nongrievers seem to accomplish with ease. But grieving means "waiting, just waiting. It's as if I'm in a distant terminal, say a bus station in Omaha, sitting, standing, and walking back and forth between the newsstand and a candy machine, unable to make any decisions about what to read or what to do" (Broyard 2005, 55). But the reporter believes his bus will come, that God will send it. His faith translates into hope: he is *waiting hopefully.* That is why he will go on to counsel *waiting patiently* in lines 25 and 29.

The Wounded Healer's Sermon (3:25–39)

His introductory testimony over, the reporter turns preacher and comes to his sermon. The sermon, which eventually extends to line 51, has features of wisdom teaching, but its content ranges widely over Old Testament traditions. Plöger has noted its closeness to Psalm 34, a didactic poem influenced by wisdom thinking. Previously wounded like the congregation and having recognized in his survival the seeds of his own healing, the preacher wants to be the means of their beginning to heal. He longs for the listening congregation to lay hold of hope for themselves. Once, I recall, at the close of a pastoral visit a patient said to me, "You have given me back my hope." For the preacher, the test of such a conviction will be whether the congregation will be prepared to pray for change.

(9) 25 Yahweh is good to the one who waits patiently for
   him,
      to the person who resorts to him.

102

²⁶It is good to be both hopeful and quiet,
    anticipating Yahweh's saving help.
²⁷It is good for a man to carry
    the yoke even when young,

⁽¹⁰⁾ ²⁸to sit alone in quietness
    because Yahweh has placed it on him,
²⁹to bite the dust—
    perhaps patient waiting will turn into reality—
³⁰to offer his cheek to the striker
    and get a lot of insults.

⁽¹¹⁾ ³¹The reason why is that the Lord's rejection
    does not last forever.
³²Rather, he brings suffering and then has compassion
    in line with his abundant grace.
³³In fact he does not want to afflict people
    or make them suffer.

⁽¹²⁾ ³⁴Crushing underfoot
    all the prisoners in the country,
³⁵violating human rights
    in front of the Most High,
³⁶mishandling persons' cases
    are what the Lord looks at, doesn't he?

⁽¹³⁾ ³⁷Who spoke and it came to be?
    The Lord ordered it, didn't he?
³⁸Did there not come from the Most High's mouth
    both misfortunes and good fortune?
³⁹Why should anyone still alive protest,
    any man, about the punishment of his sins?

The sermon is a series of persuasive arguments that prefaces the
appeal for repentant prayer in stanza 14. The sermon's generalities
are meant for the listening congregation to apply to themselves.
In the context of the complete liturgy, the positive arguments that
will be presented complete the process of attaching meaning to the
catastrophe in 586 BCE, for which the first two poems presented the
negative interpretation. As line 38 will eventually state, *misfortunes*

were the precursor of *good fortune*. Reframing the event and its aftermath with such overall meaning was intended as a coping mechanism for overwhelming grief. It had the potential to lower the anxiety level of the still-suffering congregation by changing their closed pattern of thinking and opening a way of hope. It was capable of embracing the worst and moving beyond it.

There is a smooth glide from testimony to sermon in the description of Yahweh as *good* in line 25, because divine goodness moves in the same theological orbit as the grace, compassion, and faithfulness of stanza 8, as a glance at Psalms 25:6–10; 86:5, 15; or 145:8–9 will show. In distinction from the other terms, however, here it has a future orientation, as a promise to be kept eventually in the *saving help* of the next line. Still, it is inextricably linked with present responses to God, patient waiting for that help, which must come to the surface as prayer. Resorting to or seeking God has the connotation of prayer, as in Psalm 77:2.

In the Hebrew, the three lines of stanza 9 all begin with the same word, *good*, as part of the alphabetic acrostic. In this case, not merely a letter but a word is strikingly repeated. Divine goodness in the first line is made the motivation for good human reactions to suffering in the next two. The triple reference is consciously and riskily blatant. Earlier the preacher had spoken of pre-suffering *good fortune* in line 17, and later he will mention post-suffering *good fortune* in line 38. But what can be good about present suffering? It is a hard message for sufferers to hear, and true empathy will always be sensitive to this difficulty. Sufferers are crammed so full of negativity that it is terribly difficult to find room for anything positive. They are enmeshed in their world of grief and identify with it in so many ways, even while it remains for them an alien and unbearable world. The preacher provocatively challenges this mind-set, taking further his testimony in which he has appreciated his own survival. He hopes to influence the congregation, after showing them he has been a fellow sufferer.

But such positive words as *good* are still hard to hear. Is God good? "The word 'good,' applied to Him, becomes meaningless: like abracadabra," complained C. S. Lewis (1976, 37). Ann Weems has also sounded an alarm: "No one can tell me / any good can come / from this torment! / Let them have their say / if it makes them feel better! / But I don't want / to hear it!" (1995, 99). Do sufferers wince at the title of Gerald Sittser's book, which defines his suffering as *A Grace Disguised*? If so, as they read about the intensity of his pain and recognize a fellow sufferer, one hopes that they are mollified and encouraged to move forward in their own time. Then "slowly, gradually something that could be called normal tiptoes back. And with it the faintest notion, once inadmissible, that something good would stagger out of the wreckage" (Erdal 2005, 121).

The second line of the stanza implicitly contrasts a good approach to suffering with a bad approach. The bad approach is defined in two ways, if we read the text as mirror language. First, it involves a lack of hope. The preacher applies to the congregation the lesson he has learned for himself and taught in his testimony, to move beyond the old, closed mind-set of backward-looking despair and cultivate a positive attitude. He commends to them that paradigm shift and in so doing moves beyond merely appreciating his survival as God's gift to being open to better prospects. The second way a bad approach is inferred is as the opposite of quiet endurance. What he means is deliberately and suspensefully delayed until line 39, where in rhetorical contrast to the immediately following prayer of repentance he will deprecate any shout of defiant protest that refuses to take moral responsibility for one's own suffering. Ezekiel 18 is devoted to addressing such a reaction emanating from the exiles in Babylonia, a vehement reaction that claims "the way of the Lord is not just" (Ezek. 18:25). Instead, the prophet urges repentance (Ezek. 18:30–31). In the same vein, the preacher advocates for the community a prayerful admission of their guilt that is in this respect quiet in spirit, which he will urge in line 41 and spell out in line 42 and the accompanying lament. But let there be no confusion. By no means is the preacher speaking out against that prayer or against the loud and tearful prayer that he urged Zion to utter in stanzas 18–19 of the second poem and that she did utter in stanzas 20–22. Berges compares the representation of Job as not letting protest cross his lips (Job 1:22; 2:10).

As an incentive the preacher dangles before the congregation the prospect of *Yahweh's saving help.* He here draws on a theological tradition that underlies the laments in the book of Psalms, the tradition that Yahweh rescues the covenant people from crisis. This tradition is enunciated in such texts as Psalms 34:17–18 and 91:14–16. True, it is a promise made to the righteous, but God is graciously prepared to accept conscience and confession in lieu of previous conduct, as confessions of sin in a few lament psalms attest as an alternative qualification, a back door to God's help.

The flow of the third line spills over into stanza 10. As in the second line, *good* has to do with one's attitude toward suffering. As always in the book of Lamentations, the special circumstances of the congregation and the prophetic interpretation of these circumstances as a divine sentence for earlier wrongdoing are in view. The preacher recalls Zion's *yoke* of punitive suffering mentioned in stanza 14 of the first poem. It is a heavy yoke for the congregation to bear, especially for young shoulders, but one that cannot justly be avoided, and so it is good even for the *young. Sit alone* echoes the sad description of Jerusalem at the opening of the first poem. The postwar occupation seems to be in view. The fifth poem (lines 14–15) will show how young men suffered then.

At first sight, the uncertainty of *perhaps* in line 29 seems to strike a wrong note, cutting across the preacher's purpose of encouragement. But Westermann, citing Amos 5:15, rightly calls it "quite in keeping with the spirit of parenesis" or exhortation (1994, 177). It aligns with a group of prophetic texts that modify an appeal for repentance with an embrace of divine sovereignty. These texts are Joel 2:14 ("Who knows?"); Amos 5:15; and Jonah 3:9 ("Who knows?"). *Perhaps* or "Who knows?" is like a time-limited offer in an advertisement. It invokes a sense of urgency by reducing the open window of opportunity. The aim is to induce immediate action. There is a chance, one that is worth the congregation's while to stir itself to take. The same shoulder-shrugging pose of uncertainty continues into the New Testament, in texts involving repentance (Acts 8:22; 2 Tim. 2:25). Here it helps to pave the way for the climactic call to repentance in stanza 14, just as lines 26 and 28 anticipated line 39 at the close of stanza 13. *Patient waiting* is regarded here as the companion of repentance. Lines 29 and 30 seem to have the postwar occupation of Judah in view again, anticipating the situation to be described in the twelfth stanza. In various ways the stage is being set for the denouement.

Does *good* still rankle? How can one speak of good? It is almost an obscene word to the ears of the grieving. At last, in the eleventh stanza, the preacher gives his formal explanation. Once again he draws on the theological resources of the Old Testament. It is part of his endeavor to assure the congregation that in such resources they may find the beginning of the healing their sick souls need. In the first two poems, a grim picture was painted of a God who held the people accountable for their wrongdoing. The depiction has been carried over into much of the third poem. In fact, *brings suffering* and *make suffer* (lines 32–33) render the Hebrew verb with a divine subject translated *made suffer* in the first poem at stanzas 5 and 12. In this characterization the poems have been true to the prophetic interpretive tradition that they honor. It is a characterization that is written into the covenant tradition by adding a moral "therefore" to divine grace: "You only have I chosen out of all the families of the earth; therefore I will punish you for all your iniquities" (Amos 3:2). Nevertheless, judgment is not the essence of Israel's God. Just as divine anger is not one of God's attributes but an event-oriented reaction to human wrongdoing, so judgment is an inevitable but not all-defining work of God. It is marked by relativity and contingency, not permanence. As the gospel song says, there is a way back to God from the dark paths of sin. The preacher broaches this resource for the people of God in preparation for his later call for repentance (stanza 14).

The lament tradition in the book of Psalms presupposes that divine grace can follow crisis. Yahweh delivers the covenant people and its individual members from crisis. Such grace is celebrated as an old lesson learned anew in a thanksgiving song (Ps. 116:5–6). And if the crisis was their fault, repentant confession is the key that God offers and requires in order to unlock such grace. Psalm 32 is another thanksgiving song that makes that clear, and its truth underlies the repentant lament of Psalm 51—and is reaffirmed in the New Testament at 1 John 1:9 ("If we confess . . ."). Psalm 116 celebrates God's grace and compassion, while the lamenting Psalm 51 appeals to them. These divine resources are available not only to saints but also to repentant sinners. It is on this latter, nuanced tradition that the preacher draws. It is also evident in the prophetic books, especially in the book of Hosea. In an exilic setting Second Isaiah claims and applies its truth, in particular at Isaiah 54:7–10. It is God's positive and passionate commitment to the covenant people, which does not allow judgment to have the last word.

The abundance of divine grace is a perennial Old Testament motif, from Exodus 34:6 onward. Here it stands over against the real but restricted grace of stanza 8. Though bare survival was admittedly minimal evidence of God's grace, much more is envisioned in Israel's theological tradition. Gottwald calls line 33 "the high water mark in Lamentations' understanding of God" (1954, 98). The divine unwillingness to punish underscores the contingent nature of divine punishment. It is a reaction constrained by human wrongs and not naturally welling up "from his heart," which is a literal rendering in line 33 behind the translation *want to*. What Peels says of divine vengeance is true in this case: "God's heart is not in the vengeance, but he does so when there is no other option" (1994, 295). The argument the preacher employs is one that Ezekiel 18:23, 32 also uses in a comparable situation, while 2 Peter 3:9 reaffirms it in yet another context of repentance. The ambivalence of yes and no, of grace and judgment, in the heart of God is poignantly expressed in Hosea 11:8–9. It is a tension that is a firm part of Israel's faith. The preacher moves from one pole of the tension to the other, knowing that he stands on solid theological ground, with which the listening congregation cannot theoretically disagree.

But are such arguments applicable to the situation? Yes, urges the preacher. Having spoken abstractly of divine compassion, he proceeds to give factually relevant examples of it in stanza 12. He has in view the overrunning of the land by enemy forces and its occupation in postwar Judah. He makes use of another tension, already encountered in the prayer at the end of the first poem. It is a tension between regarding the invasion as both just and unjust, just in terms of Judah's liability and unjust in terms of enemy excesses. The latter injustice loomed large in Judah's eyes as a legitimate grievance. It is to this heartfelt grievance that the preacher appeals. He is like the psalmist who said, "But you, O God, do see trouble and grief; you consider it to take it in hand. The victim commits himself to you" (Ps. 10:14). The preacher declares that God does care. God will bring about for Judah rehabilitation that will mean a rebalancing of the moral equilibrium. The divine title *Most High* carries with it an assurance that Yahweh is the universal, powerful God (cf. Ps. 47:2) and so well able to deal with such foreign aggression. Perhaps this redress of grievance is the most convincing argument in the preacher's repertoire because of its power to persuade the hurting congregation. If accepted, it will bring with it a strong inclination to accept the earlier arguments.

The preacher has run a theological marathon in his sermon. Could the congregation have kept up with him, we readers wonder. It is a reaction we also have to parts of Paul's letters in the New Testament, as 2 Peter 3:16 ruefully remarks. In this case we can assume that the theological resources would have been well known and instinctively recognized from religious memories and stories. "Hope is rooted in the past because we remember the mighty acts of God and our personal encounters with the transcendent" (Lester 1995, 22). The stumbling block would have been their applicability to the congregation's situation. The preacher's appeal to their grievances must have touched a deep element of their grief, which needed to be brought up into the light of day and aired. There was a good chance that their appreciation of the preacher's understanding would make them side with him.

The main part of the sermon is not yet finished. There remain to be spelled out two interpretive basics that use a series of rhetorical questions by way of challenge. First, an earlier revelation of the divine will is cited. Prophetic books and their message of judgment are evidently in view, as in stanza 17 of both the first and second poems, where the same verb of ordering occurs. Second, they are regarded as also including the promise of *good fortune*. This too appeals to the written form of prophetic revelation, since the prophetic books tend to supplement their main messages of judgment with a briefer note of post-judgment grace. There is significance in the order of *misfortunes* and *good fortune*, as Johnson (1985, 67) observes. A number of modern versions wrongly accommodate the phrase to the English idiomatic order, such as "good and bad" in the NRSV. But the pairing repeats the sequence of human suffering and divine compassion in line 32. This sequence is now traced back to the solid foundation of earlier written revelation. The threats of manifold *misfortunes* have come true; the prospect of *good fortune* remains to be fulfilled.

What should the congregation's reaction be to these interpretive basics? Certainly not to deny their accountability with respect to the *misfortunes*. Rather, they should identify with the scenario of judgment by pocketing their pride and praying a submissive prayer of confession and repentance. By this means they stand the chance of triggering God's response of compassion as a first step toward bringing about *good fortune* for themselves. Their path to a brighter future lies via their taking responsibility for the nation's guilt and appealing directly to God. No good can come from their engaging in loud denials of their guilt. And, as an extra motivation, appreciation of their own survival should encourage them to pray.

His Call to the Congregation to Pray (3:40–51)

Lines 40–47 at the end of the sermon are like an altar call. They summon the listening congregation to make their own response to God and suggest a model prayer they can use.

> (14) 40 Let us test the way we have behaved and examine it,
>> and then come back to Yahweh.
> 41 Let us lift up our hearts, not only our hands,
>> to God in heaven (saying),
> 42 "We for our part were rebellious and defiant,
>> so you for your part did not forgive.
>
> (15) 43 You enveloped us in anger and chased us,
>> killing with no mercy.
> 44 You enveloped yourself in cloud
>> so prayer could not get through.
> 45 Leftovers and rejects are what you have made us
>> to other peoples around.
>
> (16) 46 Staring openmouthed at us
>> are all our enemies.
> 47 We have encountered panic and pitfalls,
>> calamity and catastrophe."

111

> [48]Streams of water run down from my eyes
>   at "my poor people's catastrophe."
> (17) [49]My eyes will never stop welling up,
>   never pause,
> [50]until Yahweh gazes down
>   from heaven and looks.
> [51]What my eyes have seen has afflicted me with pain,
>   because of all the women in my city.

As Boase observes, "The flow of the text would suggest that [lines 40–41] are spoken by the man who turns to the audience, calling them to confession" (2006, 221n39). For this call to prayer it is helpful to compare Joel's advice to his community about dealing with their particular crisis. Joel suggested communal prayers for the priests to use at a national service (Joel 1:15; 2:17). In the second case the prayer is preceded by a call for wholehearted repentance (Joel 2:12–13). There the people's sins are not specified but are certainly assumed. Yahweh's abundant grace is mentioned as an incentive, along with the possibility of a divine response of blessing (Joel 2:14). These last two features have been covered earlier in this poem, in lines 29 and 32. At this juncture the preacher coaxes from the congregation an endorsement of the interpretive picture of their tragedy by adopting the prophetic style of God's punitive intervention and its consequences and by recognizing such intervention as well deserved.

What the preacher does have in common with Joel at this point is the assumption of prior sinning—in both cases left unclarified and to be substantiated by self-examination and here perhaps by hearing religious texts as part of the overall liturgy—and the call to sincere repentance. At this point the twelve-step Alcoholics Anonymous program cries out for comparison. The need for self-examination parallels step 4, making "a searching and fearless moral inventory of ourselves." In turn, the call for sincere repentance matches steps 5 and 6, admitting "to God, ourselves, and another human being the exact nature of our wrongs" and being "entirely ready to have God remove all these defects of character." Just as Joel counsels, "Let your broken heart show your sorrow; tearing your clothes is not enough" (Joel 2:13 GNT), so the preacher warns against going through the motions of regret. He advocates that the gesture of raised hands must be a genuine symbol of hearts raised to God. In the second poem at stanza 19, he urged Zion to pour out her heart and raise her hands in prayer; now he urges the congregation whom Zion represented to unite hand and heart.

Another correspondence with Joel is that he calls for a return to Yahweh (Joel 2:12–13). For the preacher too the way forward lies in coming back to God like prodigal sons and daughters, with confession on their lips. It is the human road to divine grace. At the earlier time of judgment, forgiveness, which lets sins go unpunished, was ruled out because of Judah's unrepentant persistence in wrongdoing. "Without confession of guilt and the sincere desire to repent such forgiveness is not possible" (Berges 2002, 215). Rebellion and defiance have been mentioned earlier in the liturgy. Zion uttered these terms in her exemplary confession in the first poem; now in this model prayer they are advocated once more. Such public confession is a necessary step toward restoring the relationship with Yahweh they have broken. Apart from repentance God could only punish.

The fifteenth stanza and most of the sixteenth provide the essence of the model prayer. If adopted, it proves that a lesson has been well learned, the lesson taught in the second poem and echoed in the preacher's testimony in the third, which interpreted disaster in the prophetic language of dire divine intervention and human consequences. *Anger* and *no mercy* echo key terms of the second poem and imply a deserved comeuppance. Divine anger over human sinning must be assuaged by a prayer of confession, as Psalm 38 exemplifies (vv. 1, 4, 18). So their earlier prayers stood no chance of being heard, like the preacher's in line 8. "Why should I forgive you?" (Jer. 5:7), Yahweh virtually said, when neither their conscience nor their confession as yet mitigated their misconduct. In the Old Testament, a cloud typically conceals even as it reveals God's presence (cf. Ps. 18:9–11), and here it ironically has only a concealing quality, as a sound barrier. The human consequences were the added suffering of humiliation, being treated as leftovers, food scraped off the plate for garbage.

The message of taking responsibility for wrongdoing is true, but not the whole truth for the preacher. The translation *panic and pitfalls, calamity and catastrophe* tries to imitate the assonance of the Hebrew pairs of nouns, which expresses the overwhelming nature of the people's suffering. This factor triggers a strong emotional reaction from the preacher. His double role as mediator between the congregation and Yahweh is costly. The pressure on him is so great that he breaks down, just as he did in his reporting role in the second poem at stanza 11. He becomes the wounded healer in Jung's sense. Again it is the realization of the prophetic presentiment of *my poor people's catastrophe* that drives him to painful empathy. It is an empathy that he longs for Yahweh to share. His tears will flow unabated, as a form of praying too deep for words. If we in turn are grieving and cannot find words to pray, we may regard tears as our prayer and ask God to look at them instead. The preacher yearns for Yahweh to pay attention, as a first step toward the compassion of which he spoke in line 32 and gave examples in lines 34–36, the divine compassion that he hopes human suffering will evoke according to Israel's theology.

While it was children's suffering that distressed the preacher in the second poem, now he gives a further warrant for his empathy, the terrible ways in which the women of the besieged and occupied city had suffered, caught up against their will in the male business of war. Perhaps the raping mentioned in the fifth poem (line 11) is especially in view, since occupation conditions have been on his mind. Is there also an underlying sense of deep regret that he and other males have been unable to carry out their traditional gender role as protectors?

This is his own grievance that the preacher brings to God. As part of a rhetoric of persuasion, he doubtless judges that he can get the congregation behind him and so lead them forward, making his determination to pray their own. Yahweh's compassion has been defined in stanza 12 in terms of countering excesses perpetrated directly or indirectly by the nation's enemies. The assurance there that *the Lord looks at* such excesses underlies the expectation here that Yahweh will *look* at this flagrant example. Like the woman in Jesus's parable in Luke 18:1–8, the preacher will wear God out, as it were, with his weeping. Then "will not God bring about justice for his chosen ones, who cry out to him day and night?"

His Testimony of Prayers of Appeal and Grievance (3:52–66)

In the last five stanzas, the preacher reverts to reporting a personal testimony, the way he began this poem.

> (18) 52 My enemies without cause
>   once hunted me down like a bird.
>   53 They put me in a pit to rob me of life
>   and threw stones at me.
>   54 Water rose above my head.
>   "I'm a dead man," I thought.
>
> (19) 55 I called out your name, Yahweh,
>   from deep down in the pit.
>   56 You heard my appeal, "Don't turn a deaf ear
>   to my cry for help, so I may get relief."
>   57 You drew near when I called you;
>   you said, "Don't be afraid."
>
> (20) 58 You took on my case, Lord,
>   became surety for my life.
>   59 You have seen my miscarriage of justice, Yahweh—
>   now judge my cause.

⁶⁰You have seen all their vindictiveness,
    all their plots involving me.

(21) ⁶¹ You have heard their contempt, Yahweh,
    all their plots against me,
  ⁶²the murmured talk of my attackers
    that confront me all the time.
  ⁶³Take notice of them, whether they are sitting or
      standing—
    I am ever the object of their ridicule.

(22) ⁶⁴ May you pay them back for their actions, Yahweh,
    matching what their own hands have done.
  ⁶⁵May you show them hardness of heart,
    putting your curse on them.
  ⁶⁶May you chase them in anger, wipe them out
    from under Yahweh's heaven.

The wounded healer tells another story about his own suffering.
It is a further testimony of his wounds, a long and winding story
that involves divine rescue and still more suffering that he brings
to God for resolution. Like the first testimony, it envisions ongoing suffering and so is a good parallel for a community that still
suffers. But unlike the first testimony, which had referred to God
in the third person, this one is dramatically couched in direct address, in preparation for the petitions he will bring in lines 59 and
63–66. As before, his account is meant as a model for the listening
congregation. In this case there are three aspects of modeling. For
those with ears to hear, it empathizes with them in their valley
of continuing grief, bids them look ahead to an upland of divine
assistance that he once experienced, and encourages them once
more to turn to God in prayer.

This testimony's basic perspective is quite different from that of
the first eight stanzas of the poem. There guilty suffering was in
view, suffering that recalled the preexilic prophets' sinister threats,
and Yahweh was the enemy. Here, however, as the testimony dis-
closes, *my enemies without cause*, human enemies, made the

116

speaker their target. In this poem the Hebrew pronoun *I* occurs as subject two times, in line 1, where the speaker is God's victim, and in line 63, where he is his enemies' victim. We discovered in the first poem a theological tension between deserved suffering that warranted moral accountability and an excess of suffering at the national enemies' hands that constituted a legitimate grievance to bring to Yahweh for resolution. A classic case of this tension, we noticed, surfaces in a prophetic passage at Isaiah 10. The third poem has been edging toward the latter pole of this tension, most recently with mention of the preacher's grievance over the women of Jerusalem, which drove him to pray for Yahweh's compassionate intervention. This closing prayer shares that sense of grievance and views God as a friend to help in a time of need. If divine *wrath* served to imply human guilt for the first testimony in the poem, the phrase *without cause* sets a tone of grievance for this second one.

The prayer is noticeably uncoordinated with the counseling in which the preacher engaged earlier in the poem. At one point, the event of answered prayer in lines 56–58, counseling does get close to the surface. Essentially, however, the reporter is ostensibly praying on his own account and continues doing so up to the end. His personal problem seems to have had no direct connection with the congregation's problems. And it is a separate lament from the guilty one meriting God's anger that he reported at the start of the poem. But the continuity with the tone of personal grievance that was sounded in line 51 and with the earlier mention of communal grievance in lines 34–36 demonstrates its fit in the train of thought. And, rather like lines 48–51, his own concern and praying are adduced with the expectation that the listening congregation will empathize with him, as Heim (1999, 163) remarks! By this means they will be subtly led forward in their own grieving. If this prayer is offered for God to hear, it is offered for the congregation to overhear. Their amens on his behalf, if voiced, will mean that the prayer story has reached their hearts, made them recognize

117

their parallel affinity with it, and so ministered to their own grief and grievance. The prayer has a horizontal quality, but only if its vertical nature is first taken with absolute seriousness.

The prayer story takes a winding course. It starts out as a prayer of praise with the value of a thanksgiving song such as we find in the Psalms, but that becomes the prelude to a lamenting prayer. The overcoming of an old crisis with God's help in lines 52–58 becomes the confident ground of appeals for help in a new crisis in lines 59–66 (Brandscheidt 1983, 47). Both crises are related to personal enemies who previously engaged and now engage again in unjust attacks on the one who prays. The crises are episodes of a continuing crisis involving the same parties. A parallel for such complexity occurs in the first of the so-called confessions of Jeremiah (Jer. 11:18–20). There the confession moves from interim thanksgiving in verses 18–19 to lament in verse 20, a lament that pleads for vengeance on the prophet's enemies. As here, a crisis that was thought resolved broke out again and required God's further intervention. In this context, the necessary advantage of such a complex prayer is that it can both testify to receiving God's saving help after beseeching it in prayer and still end appropriately by modeling prayer that asks for an answer.

Stanza 18 paints fairly traditional pictures of the pray-er's sufferings. Noticeably, the subjects of the first two lines are human enemies and not Yahweh as in the testimony that began the poem. Innocent suffering is portrayed here as a grievance to be brought to God. The simile of bird hunting is followed by a metaphor of animal hunting and then by a metaphor of drowning. The two metaphorical statements are united by a purpose of depriving of life in the first case and the prospect of perishing in the second. Lines 55–58 narrate a happy ending to the episode in tones of thanksgiving. The pray-er had been as good as dead, in a virtual underworld, which is what *pit* now means. But there was a positive turning point, like and unlike the one reported in lines 21–24. In this case

Yahweh answered his urgent prayers by becoming a present help and by means of a promise of salvation, like the oracles in Psalms 12:5 and 35:3, presumably passed on by a priest or prophet. The promise received here takes a traditional and reassuring format, that the cause for anxiety would be dealt with, as in Isaiah 41:10, 14, and implies God's support. And so, the reminiscence concludes, Yahweh acted as judge and righted a wrong. More, he acted as one who redeems—to give a more common rendering of the verb translated *became surety*. Yahweh became like a kinsman-redeemer, someone who intervenes to bail out a family member who has suffered dire loss according to Leviticus 25:25–55.

Lines 59–63 indicate that trouble flared up again from the same source. The lines frame statements appealing to the divine awareness of aspects of the enemies' malevolence with direct calls to intervene again as judge and to act on that awareness. Stanza 22 spells out what that could mean. It closes the prayer with vehement calls for justice that are typical of the lamenting psalms and are echoed in spirit by Paul's impassioned response to the persecuted Thessalonians' lament in 2 Thessalonians 1:6–9. Those who earlier would have taken life away if Yahweh had not intervened have surely forfeited their right to live. It is no coincidence that in tone the final stanza parallels Zion's model prayer at the close of the first poem. This prayer endorses that one. As the preacher prays for himself, so Zion has prayed for herself and, more important, the congregation should pray for themselves, not just nursing their grievance but bringing it to God to resolve.

The concluding phrase, *from under Yahweh's heaven*, is a punch line that intends to gather up similar phrases used earlier, *God's heaven* in line 41 and Yahweh's looking down *from heaven* in line 50. Each phrase belongs to a prayer context and brings an assurance of divine power to meet the needs of those who pray. The New Testament equivalent of this sentiment speaks of a throne: "Let us then approach the throne of grace with confidence, so that we may receive mercy and find grace to help us in our time of need" (Heb. 4:16). The forceful third-person phrase *Yahweh's heaven* corresponds to *Yahweh's day of anger* in Zion's prayer at the end of the second poem, as Berges observes, but now with a positive sense for the speaker.

In this poem a wounded healer offers his knowledge of God's ways and his experience of them in a context of suffering. At beginning and end he ministers out of his own suffering and presents himself as an object lesson. As a fellow sufferer, he points the congregation forward to a new wholeness that both he and they yearn to attain. In turn, we readers who are wounded have the potential to be wounded healers. We "can make ourselves and others understand that we already carry in us the source of our own search. This ministry can indeed be a witness to the living truth that the wound, which causes us to suffer now, will be revealed to us later as the place where God intimated his new creation" (Nouwen 1972, 97–98). The scar from our wound, though it may still ache, will provide relief for the raw pain of others. The presupposition of this new gift is not only the experience of suffering but also the maturity and new sense of identity that it can creatively bring about. A widow, reflecting on her life before her loss and after the mourning of her loss, put it this way: "But today I am someone else. I am stronger, more independent. I have more understanding, more sympathy. . . . I am a different woman" (Caine 1974, 222).

4

Fourth Poem (Lamentations 4)

Grief and Guilt Prolonged—and to Be Reversed

After the buildup of the first three poems with their ever more insistent calls to the listening congregation to pray and even, in the third poem, to indulge in hope for the future, we readers are ready for the congregation's prayer in the fifth poem. Instead, it is put on hold, and readers are brought back to more reports of the grief and guilt of the first and second poems. In particular, several topics of grief and an expression of guilt from the second poem are taken up here. Likewise, those who grieve find themselves playing and replaying their distressing memories and concerns in their minds and in talking to others.

In the fourth poem, the mentor reflects this attitude. He takes his own advice to *wait patiently*. Grieving is a large part of the waiting. He leaves unmentioned the need for prayer. It has been elaborated enough in the third poem, and readers are left in suspense. The reason why is surely that it takes time for such a message to sink in, and the fourth poem wisely gives the congregation that time lag. Grief, which is the major component of this poem, has its own timetable, lasting as long as it takes in each case. Seeds of hope have been sown in the third poem with the prospect of germinating, but it is not yet time for them to break through the ground. The final stanza of this poem will revert to the earlier message of hope, insisting that it is only a matter of time before it will come true. Until then, the healing of the wounds of grief is a slow and drawn-out process. Henri Nouwen wrote in a letter to his father about his mother's death: "Maybe these words will only increase your tears and deepen your grief. But for me, your son, who grieves with you, there is no other way. I want to comfort and console you, but not in a way that covers up real pain and avoids all wounds" (1982, 17).

The GIs who landed in Normandy in World War II and made their laborious way across Europe had a saying, that the only way home was via Berlin. There could be no shortcuts. Gerald Sittser once had a dream of trying to escape the darkness of his grief by running west to rediscover the setting sun. After he had told his sister the dream, she perceptively said, "The quickest way for anyone to reach the sun and the light is . . . to head east, plunging into the darkness until one comes to the sunrise" (1996, 33). As one grieves, it can take a long time for soul and body to absorb and neutralize the shocks and aftershocks that grief inflicts.

The fourth poem recognizes that it is still time to tell the old story and talk it out, reliving the tragedy by flashbacks as vivid as if they happened yesterday. Ann Weems speaks for the listening congregation and for many others who mourn when she writes in one of her poems, "Every waking moment is filled / with the pain of that moment" (1995, 15). Those who grieve live inside the details of their particular stories. They are left suspended in past time, a time that seems much more vivid and relevant than their present, and that suspension lasts uncomfortably long for nongrieving observers. "For the person who mourns, everything has ground to a halt. Yet he or she lives in a world that appears not to have missed a step. It is in the midst of this disparity that a grieving person withdraws from the world" (Irish 1975, 34). Kübler-Ross and Kessler have observed about grieving: "It seems strange that the clocks in the world continue when your inner clock does not" (2005, 29).

The preacher of the previous poem turns back into the reporter of the congregation's troubles, the same role he played in the first two poems. His signature is plainly visible in this poem at stanza 10, in the reference to *my poor people's catastrophe*. This phrase, full of compassion, he had uttered earlier, in the second poem (stanza 11) and the third (stanza 8). He also continues his restatement of this particular calamity in the same interpretive terms he had used before. In this way he urges his hearers to take responsibility for the communal guilt that precipitated the calamity. Their grief cannot be put to rest until their guilt is acknowledged in confession. Once more we readers sense a building up to the final prayer that both the reporter-preacher and we will be glad to hear eventually, when the time is ripe. Until then, the long wait must go on. It is not a waste of time but a needed opportunity to work through the grief and its how and why. Grief is a process. "There is no way to go over, around, or under—we must go through it" (Rando 1984, 97). I shudder when I recall what one severely depressed patient told me: "My in-laws tell me to pull myself together and get over it. My husband half supports me and half sides with them."

The structure of the fourth poem is an outworking of the demands of grief and guilt. It falls into four sections, stanzas 1–6, 7–11, 12–16, and 17–22, which neatly subdivide the two halves of the poem. In each case an expression of divine intervention that takes guilt seriously closes a long outpouring of grief, as Weiser, Droin, Berges, and Albertz (2003, 153) maintain; in the last case an ending of the guilt is envisioned. What each of these conclusions is in danger of losing by its brevity it more than regains as a climax. The alternation within the sections means that the elements of divine intervention and human consequences, a familiar feature of earlier poems based on the format of prophetic oracles, are largely maintained, but now they are put the other way round. The initial cry of the dirge, *How terrible that . . . !*, already encountered in the first two poems, returns here but now occurs not once but twice. And once more the limping meter of the Hebrew dirge predominates in this poem. The initial cries and the meter set the tone of the poem, though the refrains of responsibility toward God and its particular reinforcement in stanza 13 go beyond the human concerns of the dirge. Like a traditional dirge, the poem narrates reversals of good times into shocking sequels, so that expectations based on earlier experience are dashed. In the last stanza, however, a counter-reversal is promised. For the reporter at least, hope like that envisioned in the third poem finally replaces the predominant tone of distress, like the light of dawn dispelling the long, dark night.

The alphabetic acrostic form that proclaims the totality of grief is used once more in the Hebrew, with a fresh letter beginning each stanza, so this one is like those employed in the first two poems. It abandons the special form of the third poem, where the same letter graced each line of its stanza. But, unlike all three of the previous poems, this one has stanzas of only two lines, not three, which makes the poem a third shorter. This change is best explained as evidence of working toward a literary closure (Dobbs-Allsopp, adapting a concentric view of the book first proposed by Nägelsbach). The fifth poem will have even less of an acrostic form and consist of only twenty-two lines, not stanzas. The series of poems is gradually working down to a conclusion, signaled here by starting the shortening process.

The Cheapening of Human Life (4:1–6)

The first section, after a striking metaphorical introduction, gives two examples of suffering and finally identifies it as a tragic reaping of the wrong the community had sown.

[1]How terrible that the gold turned dull,
    the purest gold changed color,
that the sacred stones were strewn around
    at every street corner!

[2]Zion's family, once so precious
    and worth their weight in high-grade gold—
how terrible that they were valued as earthen jars
    handmade by any potter!

[3]Even jackals offer their breasts
    to suckle their whelps,
but my people's womenfolk turned as cruel
    as wild ostriches.

[4]Babies' tongues stuck fast
    to the roofs of their thirsty mouths.
Young children pleaded for bread,
    but nobody could give them a piece.

[5]People who once ate luxury foods
    lay devastated in the streets.
Those brought up to wear purple
    hung around the ash heaps.

[6]My poor people's punishment for their wrongdoing
        was greater
    than Sodom's for its sin,
which was overthrown virtually in a moment
    with no (human) hands turned against it.

The section opens with a pair of stanzas that together sum up the poem's reason for grief and individually move from imagery to underlying meaning. This symmetry is evident from the double repetition, not only of *gold* but also of the shriek that is characteristic of the dirge, *ekhah* in Hebrew, "that sound which is both inhuman and guttural and the most human sound a person can make: the sound of grief" (Hood 2008, 150). My rendering *How terrible that . . . !* loses its brevity but tries to convey its stark emotion. *Ekhah* occurs here in the book for the last time, its doubling an echo of the single cries at the head of the first two poems.

A visual counterpart to the cry is the painting *The Scream* by the expressionist artist Edvard Munch. The artist portrays himself against the background of an uncannily lurid sunset over land and water. The luridness was perhaps caused by debris drifting from the volcanic eruption at Krakatoa in Indonesia in 1883 (Drapkin and Zielinski 2009, 75). He stands alone, with gaping mouth and staring eyes, holding his hands over his ears to try to shut out the shrill scream of nature he perceives around him, which the personal anguish he felt at the time picked up and responded to. In earlier poems the reporter has spoken of the groaning of his inanimate environment, with which his groans of despair were an empathic link. Perhaps Weems captures the thought: "The whole world is / one great wailing wall / and I will live here / forever!" (1995, 70). In the New Testament, a parallel appears in Paul's double lament about nature's groaning for eschatological renewal, groaning that suffering Christians match with the groans of their own hearts (Rom. 8:22–23).

The cries are set in a general flashback that sums up the grim experiences of those shut up in Jerusalem during the siege. Those experiences will be elaborated gradually in the following sections by singling out various groups of victims of extreme suffering. The fourth poem develops the references to such groups introduced at times in the course of the second poem. Personification of Zion appears only at the beginning and end of the poem. Its place is taken by detailed realities of human suffering. The reporter narrates a series of street scenes in the first eighteen stanzas. *At every street corner* launches the series. Its continuation will be signaled in each of the four sections in turn by *in the streets* in stanzas 5, 8, and 14 and *in our squares* in stanza 18. It is a motif that in the second poem appeared in two clusters, at stanzas 11, 12, 19, and 21. Here it is developed into a regular feature, creating a series of stations along the poem's Via Dolorosa.

The general introduction of the first two stanzas bemoans the utter devaluation of human worth during the siege. There is a lack of clarity about the images. First, gold does not tarnish, as the Hebrew is generally understood. Is this poetic panache that does not matter (Reyburn)? Or is its normal impossibility presupposed, as a mark of the severity of this abnormal situation (Gous 1996, 81; Dobbs-Allsopp; Berges)? Or is a covering of dirt intended instead (Berlin), specifically blackening from smoke (Plöger)? Second, what are the *sacred stones*? They seem to correspond to the adjective *precious* in the explanation, in an unfolding from symbol to substance. If so, they probably refer to jewels. One of the functions of a temple in the ancient Near East was to be a treasury, and this function may be in view here, a depository for jewelry. Gold and jewelry, usually treated with the respect they warranted, here almost take on the valuelessness of trash. This was how human lives fared, with a gross lack of respect. Life, normally as safeguarded and highly valued as gold, by a perverse kind of alchemy became as cheap and expendable as a clay pot. Such pots were a dime a dozen, and a broken pot was easily replaced. The reporter's reaction is one of anguish. By contrast, two psalms affirm the essential value of human life. In Psalm 72:14, the good king rescues his subjects from potentially fatal oppression and violence because "their blood" is "precious" or, better, too costly "in his sight." And in Psalm 116:15, God typically rescues any among the covenant people who are threatened by death because "precious" or too costly "in the sight of the LORD is the death of his saints." Here, however, this basic principle of human worth was shockingly denied.

The first specific picture of suffering during the siege occupies stanzas 3 and 4. It returns to the haunting memory recalled in the second poem, in stanzas 11 and 12, portraying the thirst and hunger of young children whose piteous crying had to go unanswered. Children were normally breastfed up to the age of three (cf. 2 Macc. 7:27). In this case, their mothers' dry breasts could not satisfy them with what their empty stomachs craved, so that their *tongues* did not stick *fast to* the breasts but to the roofs of their own mouths instead (Berges). There is an ironic playing with the unnaturalness of such treatment. It looked as if the mothers were cruel and the way they were forced to treat their children was inhuman. Even animals nurse their young. These mothers looked as bad as ostriches, which folklore credited with abandoning their eggs and neglecting their chicks (Job 39:14–16). Young life represented the next generation. So the long-term survival of the community was brought to a tragic end by deprivation unwillingly inflicted by those who were powerless to help. And on a personal level, what is a worse bereavement to bear than losing a child? It perversely defies an expectation that the parent will be the first to die and cruelly kills myriad hopes and dreams along with the child. C. S. Lewis (1976, 29) perceptively observed that a mother mourns for what her child has lost, not just for what she has lost. William Wordsworth in his poem "Surprised by Joy" described the death of his four-year-old daughter as "the worst pang that sorrow ever bore, / . . . when I stood forlorn, / Knowing my heart's treasure was no more."

Stanza 5 looks briefly at another reversal, this time from riches to rags. But once more the accent is on food. Just as starving inmates of a concentration camp obsess about food, here lack of food is siege talk again. Rags also find an implicit place, in contrast to robes made of expensive, dyed material these wealthy citizens used to wear before the long siege impoverished them (cf. Luke 16:19). The providential blessing of upward mobility from ash heap to prosperity in 1 Samuel 2:8 and Psalm 113:7 finds a terrible reversal here. In stanza 6, the reporter moves from bare facts to their interpretation. He discovers no room for grievance here, but with a blend of frankness and compassion—even the guilty need compassion—he compares and contrasts the final siege of Jerusalem with the destruction of another city, Sodom. Ancient Israelite lore credited its wickedness as the cause and God as the agent of its overthrow (Gen. 18–19). The prophet Isaiah a century before this siege had bluntly compared the capital's moral state with that of Sodom and Gomorrah (Isa. 1:10). In the same way, Jerusalem's plight is here traced back to the people's wrongdoing as its true cause, in prophetic mode. Just as divine intervention held Sodom accountable for its wickedness, so Jerusalem's suffering during the siege was to be explained. However, the people's suffering could be described as worse, since Zion's destruction was enacted in agonizingly slow motion rather than with relatively merciful suddenness. Stanza 9 will say something similar, from a different perspective. The listening congregation must accept the blame for what were human consequences not simply of divine intervention but also of the wrongdoing that underlay it.

More Horrors of the Siege (4:7–11)

This next section has no need of the introduction in the first one but otherwise traces the same pattern: the replaying of two grim experiences of starvation during the siege and a closing theological interpretation. In describing this deadly situation, it appropriately draws once more on the dirge's contrast between earlier prosperous normality and the rigors of the siege.

> ⁷Her leaders once looked more lustrous than snow,
>   more wholesome than milk.
> Their bodies were ruddier than corals
>   the figure they cut as appealing as lapis lazuli.
>
> ⁸They came to look blacker than soot,
>   going unrecognized in the streets.
> Their skin shriveled on their bones,
>   turning dry as wood.
>
> ⁹Victims of the sword were better off
>   than the victims of hunger,

129

who wasted away and were dispatched
  by lack of produce from the countryside.

[10]With their own hands compassionate women
  cooked their children,
who became their food
  during "my poor people's catastrophe."

[11]Yahweh discharged the full force of his fury,
  the flood of his burning anger,
and set ablaze in Zion a fire
  that consumed her foundations.

Grief takes the color out of life. Berlin has perceptively drawn attention to the rhetorical use of color in the first two sections: the yellow of gold, the purple of exotic robes, the bright white of snow and milk, the red of corals, and the sparkling blue of lapis lazuli. They are all replaced by the blackness of soot. Movies sometimes use the technique of switching between Technicolor and black and white to accentuate quite different experiences, for example in *The Wizard of Oz*. Here the rainbow of fresh colors fades to a somber black, registering the switch from good times to grief-laden scenes. Weems makes a parallel use of this imagery and even of its dirge background to describe how she perceived her world in her own period of grief: "O God, / the world has been drained / of color! / The music has been turned off! / The silent shroud / covers any green that remains. / All is grey / and smells of death" (1995, 16).

The dirgelike reversal is laid out in stanzas 7 and 8. People in the top echelons of national and urban government once reflected their power in their physical appearance. They were each a picture of glowing health, with their attractive, copper-toned skin, and each a focus of public attention, as eye-catching as a sparkling jewel. Plöger has compared the flattering picture of manhood lovingly drawn in Song 5:10–16. But all that changed during the siege; they merged unnoticed with the public they had previously impressed. As in line 10 of the fifth poem, blackness seems to have been an effect of starvation. "Everyone is now blue-black, bloodless," reads a report of hunger in the siege of Leningrad during World War II (Jones 2008, 228). The people of Jerusalem came to resemble concentration-camp prisoners whom we readers have seen staring out of old newsreels or pictures in history books. Their wasted, wizened state leads to a generalization about their suffering in stanza 9 that reinforces the sixth stanza. Both direct conflict with the enemy and the indirect state of siege brought about death sooner or later, but the lingering death from starvation in the latter case made the former preferable. Cut off from crops in the fields outside the city, the people were doomed. It is typical of long sieges that famine is the major cause of death.

The next example of reversal, in stanza 10, is briefly told but is the most shocking of all, a story of incredible horror that develops the even briefer mention in stanza 20 of the second poem. To be sure, there is no reason to speculate that this is the sort of cannibalism in which humans are killed and eaten, as Kraus and Brandscheidt (1983, 177) maintain. The text speaks only of necrophagia, the eating of cadavers already dead from other causes. Traditional respect for the dead and abhorrence of what was ritually unclean (Num. 19:11) were trumped by the instinct of survivors to stay alive. The atrocity of this stanza finds a place in the siege description in Deuteronomy 28:53–57, which is echoed in Jeremiah 19:9. However, unlike the second poem, there is no overlap in vocabulary here to suggest the reporter's intention to specifically remind his listeners of either passage. Eating the dead is a ghastly commonplace in siege accounts, ancient and modern. One sad story of American pioneering days involves a struggle for survival that necessitated eating human flesh. Those in the Donner Party who were snowbound in the mountains, as they traveled across America in their covered wagons making for California in the winter of 1846–47, ate their dead companions to stay alive. As the nine-hundred-day siege of Leningrad in World War II—a siege twice as long as the one that Jerusalem probably endured—wore on, the scarcity of food drove some people to kill and more to take gruesome advantage of unburied corpses, even selling human flesh on the black market (Jones 2008, 215–19, 242).

Commentators interpret *compassionate* as a pre-siege trait, which fits the overall focus on reversal. However, even during the siege, mothers had lovingly held their dying children in their arms, according to stanza 12 of the second poem, giving them what meager comfort they could in their final moments. Women are dramatically pinpointed in this version of eating human flesh. Cooking is a service for the family. Once as compassionate to their living and dying children as mothers could ever be, now they practiced their domestic routine of cooking for the family on the dead flesh of those children to prolong the lives of members of the family who were still alive. Does *compassionate* include their continuing care for family survivors, which in an already surreal world had the power to supersede cultural conventions? Extremity can reverse priorities; here it causes a clash of feminine instincts. What was a woman to do? The reporter's implicit posing of this question exacerbates the horror and explains it as a dilemma. As at times in earlier poems, he has a keen eye for women's concerns and finds them emotionally stirring, as doubtless the listening congregation was meant to do.

The reporter's use of *my poor people's catastrophe* as a prophetic quotation in stanza 11 of the second poem and line 48 of the third suggests that the same applies here and that this phrase is intended to prompt and prepare for the oracle-like divine intervention of the next stanza. Personal compassion and providential inevitability are both at stake in the phrase. There is naturally an emotional wringing of hands that such an atrocity should have occurred. But there is also a challenge to get beyond emotion to the interpretive insight of the eleventh stanza. The stories of stanzas 7–10 are nothing less than the human consequences of the terrible divine intervention that was comprehensively forecast by the preexilic prophets. The intervention is evoked with the imagery of an all-consuming fire of fury, repeated from stanzas 3 and 4 of the second poem.

When no food was left, fire came and found food of its own to gobble up. The rhetorical bonding of the concluding stanza with the previous ones is achieved by the motif of eating. Renkema (1988, 337), Gous (1996, 82), and Berges draw attention to this link. During the siege, eating was eventually ruled out for humans, as food supplies were exhausted, but in its immediate aftermath, when the city was captured, eating was ironically realized in another sense, in the consuming or eating up of Jerusalem's foundations. The rhetorical irony conveys a message of the essential connection between what happened and why it happened.

As in the second poem, *fury* or *anger* functions not as a divine initiative but as a reflex to unacceptable human behavior for which the people had to be held accountable. The vehemence of the divine reaction to this underlying factor matches the passion of the previous stories. Fire does connect with the fire of enemy destruction after the city fell, but it is basically metaphorical since foundations cannot literally be destroyed by fire. The metaphor illustrates the radical form that tragedy can take. Friedrich Schleiermacher preached a sermon at his son Nathanael's grave, affirming that "this one blow . . . has shaken my life to its roots" (2006, 148). In Jerusalem's case, its end brought to a finale some basic principles on which the capital was established and which the remaining two sections of the poem will separately mention. So the second line of stanza 11 functions as a virtual headline for those sections, which make up the second half of the poem. What are those principles? Stanza 12 will highlight the value accorded to Jerusalem in the theology of Zion, while stanza 20 will focus on the value set on the Davidic monarchy. These two traditions were the city's veritable foundations that were tragically consumed by the divine reflex to Judah's culpability.

How One Guilty Group Suffered (4:12–16)

The third section of the poem is like the two earlier sections in having a closing stanza that brings Yahweh into the picture. But it lacks their twin cameos of suffering during the siege, a long one followed by a short one. Instead, it moves from a stanza of general reversal relating to the fall of the city (stanza 12), to an explanation in terms of the moral accountability of a particular group of citizens for the fall (stanza 13), and then to the report of a series of sufferings this group experienced as a consequence (stanzas 14–16).

> [12]Kings worldwide could not believe it,
>> nor could the rest of humankind,
> that a foe, an enemy, would ever come
>> through Jerusalem's gates,
>
> [13](which happened) because of the sins of her
>> prophets,
>> the wrongs of her priests,
> who spilled inside her walls
>> the blood of the innocent.
>
> [14]They wandered blindly in the streets,
>> defiled with blood.
> What they were forbidden (to touch)
>> they touched with their clothes.
>
> [15]"Get away! Unclean!"
>> people shouted at them.
> "Get away! Get away! Don't touch us!"
>> In fact, fleeing, they wandered around,
> told by other nations
>> they could stay with them no longer.
>
> [16]Yahweh himself dispersed them.
>> no longer showing regard for them.
> They showed the priests no respect,
>> even aged ones no favor.

A motif of dirgelike reversal appears once more in the first stanza of this third section. A terrible reversal had befallen Jerusalem. It had traditionally been hailed as the city of God in Psalms 47:4; 48:1–2; and 87:2. These psalms, along with Psalm 76, are generally called songs of Zion. They express the theological value of Zion as special and impregnable, ever protected by the God who was present in its temple. Earlier in the book, the second poem had cited this theology at stanza 15, in terms of a reversal, contrasting the beauty of the blessed city with the ruinous condition to which it had been reduced. Now there is another allusion to this tradition. Psalm 76:11–12, as a corollary of Zion's unique role, urges "all the neighboring lands" to "bring gifts to the One who is to be feared" and states that "he is to be feared by the kings of the earth." This Zion-related obligation and awe are here taken with complete seriousness (Albrektson 1963, 226). The rest of the world must surely react to Jerusalem's conquest with incredulous surprise. Implicitly, it was for the city no less than a fall from grace. It was indeed an *astounding downfall*, as the first poem put it in stanza 9. Behind the enhancement lies the challenge it brought to the congregation's faith in the God of Zion, which must have initially taken the form of shocked disbelief. "I can't believe it's true" is a common early response to loss.

This shocking reversal cries out for an explanation, which is supplied in stanza 13. Blame is laid at the door of the stewards of Zion theology, the inner circle among its citizens, who represented Yahweh by prophecy and priestly service. In Israel's history, according to 1 Samuel 2–3, the punishment of the wicked priests Hophni and Phinehas entailed the Philistines' capture of the sacred ark. Similarly, the brash irresponsibility of Zion's prophets and priests had dragged Zion down. Presumably the prophets—the same ones as in the second poem at stanza 14, which is presupposed here—are envisioned as those who had reassuringly appealed to Zion theology as the charm that would guarantee peace and rule out calamity, as

Jeremiah 14:13 and 23:17 suggest. The priestly establishment went along with this convenient hermeneutic: "prophets prophesy lies and priests are in league with them" (Jer. 5:31 REB). The killing of the innocent seems to refer to the fatal effect of this policy in general, after Jerusalem fell. These prophets and priests bore ultimate responsibility for the city's casualties at the enemy's hands. However, *sins* and *wrongdoing* appear to have been committed directly by the religious group, in line with the moral accusations of Jeremiah 23:11, 14. The unfaithfulness of Yahweh's stewards trumped their theology, venerable though it was, exposing it as an empty tradition that Yahweh could no longer uphold.

Evidently the fate of this group is disclosed step by step in stanzas 14–16. The reference to *priests* in stanza 16 seems to provide closure for the report. In fact, these stanzas focus on the priestly component of the group, as the allusions to ritual purity in stanzas 14 and 15 show. If *the blood of the innocent* in the previous stanza does refer to post-siege casualties, such a time frame also fits stanzas 12 and 14. Amid the melee of conquest the priests became contaminated by the bloodshed and were no longer able to maintain their ritual purity. Ironically, they became the butt of calls from nonpriestly folk to keep away as unclean, as if they were lepers or the like (cf. Lev. 13:45). This ostracism followed them as they fled as refugees to neighboring states, where they found themselves equally unwanted, though presumably not for the same reason. The closing stanza traces all this rejection back to Yahweh: it was the human consequences of divine intervention in reprisal for their wrongdoing, it is implied. The final line reverts to a further consequence, their disrespectful treatment at the hands of the nations with whom they had tried to find refuge. Gone was their high status, forfeited by their willfulness.

Reversal has loomed large in this section—not only reversal of a theological tradition but also of the priests' cultic purity and of their social status. Suffering has also been featured, but very much guilty suffering. Grief has a lesser role but is perceptible, grief over the shocking loss of a prized theological tradition and over the sad collapse of the religious establishment, deserved though it was.

Despair—and Eventual Hope (4:17–22)

In the last section, two more cameos of past suffering are presented in tones of grief in stanzas 17–18 and 19–20, each accompanied by a reversal of great expectations. Failed expectation and factual experience are set in an ABB'A' framework that draws attention to the disappointments. The poem concludes in stanzas 21 and 22 with a counter-reversal of triumphant expectation that deals with a sore grievance and promises justice.

> ^{17}Our eyes were strained continually,
>> waiting "in vain" for "help" to reach us.
> From our watchtower we watched
>> for a nation that could not save us.
>
> ^{18}They tracked our steps
>> so we could not walk in our squares.
> Our end got close, our lives were over,
>> yes, our end had come.
>
> ^{19}Those who chased us were faster
>> than eagles in the sky,
> in hot pursuit over the mountains,
>> ambushing us in the wilderness.
>
> ^{20}The very breath in our nostrils, Yahweh's anointed one,
>> was captured in their traps—
> he under whose protective shadow we had thought
>> we would thrive among the other nations.
>
> ^{21}Cheer and laugh, Lady Edom,
>> you who live in the region of Uz.

> Your turn is coming to have the cup passed on to
>   you.
> You will get drunk and strip yourself naked.
>
> [22]The punishment for your wrongdoing will end,
>   Lady Zion;
> he will keep you in exile no longer.
> He will deal with your wrongdoing, Lady Edom,
>   uncovering your sins.

A striking difference from the earlier sections is shown in the first-person plural reports that seem to anticipate the voice of the community in the fifth poem. From one perspective this is a bridging device that embraces the community before it takes over the speaking. The last two stanzas do appear to be spoken by the speaker of the third poem. Accordingly, the reporter is here speaking with a new inclusivity, instead of describing the suffering as that of *my (poor) people*, as in stanzas 3, 6, and 10. Another incentive for the switch is that stanza 19 seems to represent an eyewitness account that the reporter could give as a member of a particular group. From this perspective, the previous cameo in the section was attracted into that format for the sake of continuity. The new format affirms his involvement with the listening people as one who had shared their suffering.

The first cameo begins with the dashing of hope in stanza 17. The time frame reverts to the period of siege. Grief is often aggravated by severe disappointment that a tragedy brings with it, such as the death of a young person in whom parents had invested hopes for the future. After Ann Weems lost her son on his twenty-first birthday, she wrote, "My dreams, O God, / are gone. / Dead / buried / one after another / gone forever . . . / Am I to be buried / with them? / When dreams die / does the / dreamer / die / with them?" (1995, 93). Here the disappointment that strained the eyes was being let down by allies. It was one of the community's rawest wounds, as its early appearance in the book, in stanza 2 of the first poem, attests. Commentators usually see here a reference to Egypt, which would fit the failed attempt of the Egyptian army to come to Judah's aid in 587 BCE (see Jer. 37:5–11). Renkema (1988, 346) and Berlin suggest that there is a deliberate reference to Isaiah's indictment of Egypt in Isaiah 30:7, where the same Hebrew words for *in vain* and *help* occur. History was repeating itself. Perhaps reflection added bitterness to the emotional mix. Was not Egypt ever a broken reed (Isa. 36:6)?

Stanza 18 looks back to the danger faced by those cooped up in the capital during the closing days of the siege. They had to avoid certain areas that were within shooting range of the enemy (Streane, Kraus). The siege descriptions of Ezekiel 4:2 and 21:22 shed light on this text. The enemy put battering rams in place outside the city gates, which adjoined public squares. Alongside the rams they set tall, wheeled siege towers ("siege works"; REB, "towers") manned by archers who gave fire support to the soldiers operating the rams (Yadin 1963, 314–15, 391). They shot at the defenders on the walls and gate buildings and could fire into the squares. This escalation of the siege filled the besieged with fresh fear and with a demoralized foreboding that gave up on life. There may be an allusion to Amos 8:2 (NRSV), "The end has come upon my people Israel."

Another cameo of suffering in stanzas 19 and 20 was unforgettably imprinted on the victims' minds. This one moves to the next, nightmarish stage, when the city finally fell. To avoid capture and massacre, the military defenders slipped out of an exit of Jerusalem that was not under attack and fled east over the mountains, evidently hoping to reach and cross the Jordan to relative safety. They represent a parallel to the priestly fugitives in stanza 15, who managed to flee to neighboring states. Second Kings 25:4–5 and Jeremiah 52:7–8 describe the episode with more factual detail, but this account conveys the emotional dimension of the chase. Readers, as before, can sense the demoralization and despair that anticipated capture and can almost hear the thumping of overstrained hearts.

Among the fugitives was King Zedekiah, who found himself isolated and taken prisoner. A shock wave of disappointment reverberates all through stanza 20. Perhaps it is matched in the Bible only by the heartbroken regret of the Emmaus-bound disciples over another *anointed one* or Messiah: "We had hoped that he was the one who was going to redeem Israel" (Luke 24:21). Indeed, the book of Lamentations has been theologically dated on "the Holy Saturday of Israel's life, caught between exilic death at the hands of Babylon and the desperate, though fragile, hope for resurrection" (Parry 2006, 410). The stanza begins and ends with a sort of eulogy. Weak king though he was, Zedekiah was nevertheless a representative of the traditional Davidic monarchy, the God-given focus of vitality, stability, and protection for his subjects. The eulogies are somewhat like the lavish royal ideals set out in Psalm 89:19–37, which the realism of "but . . ." cuts across and kills. In some of the narratives about David, the role of the king of Israel as God's anointed arouses awesome respect for someone who is sacrosanct and should be beyond human harm (1 Sam. 24:10; 26:9, 16; 2 Sam. 1:14, 16). Here, however, such an aura was absent. This expression of disappointed expectation, alongside stanza 12 in the previous section, mentions another part of the fundamental infrastructure of the community's existence that had become fuel for the fire of divine anger, according to the imagery of the eleventh stanza. Zion, not only as the religious center of the nation but also as the royal capital, was doubly lost to its flames.

The reporter thinks he can hear laughter, offstage as it were. We readers can imagine him cupping his hand to his ear. It is a mocking laughter that aggravates the community's private grief with a secondary factor, humiliation from the ridicule of others. This extra feature was regularly bemoaned in earlier poems, in particular the enemy's cheering in the first poem (stanza 21) and laughter in the second (stanza 17). At the end of the first poem it initiated a sense of grievance that was expressed as Zion's prayer

140

for justice to be done. It is a measure of the development in the series of poems that now the grievance is framed as the reporter's statement of future fact, as a claim of what God will definitely do. Let those who laugh do so while they still can! The last laugh will be not theirs but God's. "The One enthroned in heaven laughs; the Lord scoffs at them" (Ps. 2:4). Zion too will be enabled to laugh, it is implied, in a reversal of her grief. This is a counter-reversal for Zion, signaled by two repetitions of vocabulary used negatively earlier in the poem but positively here. *Punishment for wrongdoing* reappears from stanza 6 and *no longer* from stanzas 15 and 16. Zion's grievance will be taken seriously; justice will be done. The confident tone leans back on the assurances given in the third poem. The verb *end* in stanza 22 has been used only once before in the book, in line 22 of the third poem, *Yahweh's gracious acts have not ended*. There it celebrated the reporter's survival, while here it takes on a broader significance for Zion and so for the community.

The reporter recognizes Edom as the one who laughs and rhetorically addresses the national enemy as a woman, *Lady Edom*, a foil to *Lady Zion*, who will soon reappear. The issue is not just mockery over Jerusalem's downfall but a slew of *wrongdoing* and *sins*, which are left unexplained. Elsewhere Edom, Judah's neighbor to the southeast, is represented as an archenemy in the historical context of Judah's war with Babylon, in Psalm 137:7 and throughout the book of Obadiah, where Edom is accused of treachery against Judah by allying itself with Judah's enemy. That grievance is evidently reflected here. It echoes the grievance expressed at the end of the first poem, but whereas there only enemies in general are mentioned, here the enemy is pinpointed. And whereas there the grievance was expressed as a prayer, here it is translated into a confident statement of future fact. Moreover, whereas there the need for justice used the prophetic metaphor of the day of the Lord, as a comprehensive term for God's judgment day for all nations, here another prophetic metaphor is used that has a similar import,

141

Yahweh's cup of wrath that each nation has to drink and suffer its dire effects—like Noah's drunken experience in Genesis 9:21, but worse. The metaphor occurs in a variety of texts, including Obadiah 15–16, where Edom, among other nations, is promised the cup that the Judeans had already drunk on Yahweh's "holy hill." The metaphor is developed at great length in Jeremiah 25:15–29. Here the metaphor is translated into straightforward meaning in the second half of stanza 22.

But that is not the only way that justice will be seen to be done. *Lady Edom* and *Lady Zion* are polarized as rivals in the closing pair of stanzas. *Lady Zion* fleetingly reappears from the first and second poems, for the last time. The reporter was unable to bring any words of comfort to her when he addressed her in stanza 13 of the second poem, but now he can. The polarization takes the form of a seesaw effect. While Edom will come down, Zion will shoot up in her fortunes. Often in the prophetic literature bad news for Israel's enemies is accompanied by good news for Israel, for example in Malachi 1:2–5 concerning Edom and Judah again. The red light for Edom, as it were, signals a green light for Zion in the cross street. The first half of stanza 22 is devoted to this green light that the reporter can glimpse in Zion's future, a termination of her punishment at Yahweh's hands and an end set on her guilt. It is spoken against the background of the third poem, as a restatement of the assurances he gave the congregation in lines 31 and 32 there, that divine rejection does not last forever and that compassion follows suffering. The drawing of exile to a close reverses Judah's exile in line 3 of the first poem. The mention of Zion here appears to embrace the compatriots of the listening congregation who had been exiled.

Most of the fourth poem has been devoted to bemoaning memories of loss in the manner of a dirge for the dead. So much of the community's previous life had died, as it were, amid Jerusalem's experiences of siege and conquest. The reporter has once more articulated in the poem the congregation's sense of being bereaved. He has used flashbacks to this end, as a necessary part of the processing of their grief. "We must allow the film to roll, and dare to watch it" (Fumia 2000, 104). But in the conclusion of the poem he switches to a flash-forward because he is moving in spirit to a lament psalm, in particular to an affirmation of confidence that was a regular component of such a psalm. One form an affirmation of confidence takes is to envision a future action of God, for example in Psalm 55:23, "But you, O God, will bring down the wicked into the pit of corruption." Stanza 22 takes this form, though in a lament psalm it would typically, but not always, be addressed to God. This one speaks of God in the third person, as does Psalm 27:10, "Though my father and mother forsake me, the LORD will receive me." It expresses an assurance that the psalm's prayer for help would be answered. In this case, grief and grievance, all-engrossing though they now are, will give way to hope and justice, and the price for guilt will be adequately paid. In each area of burdensome concern, God can be trusted.

The reporter, implicitly depending on his sermon in the third poem, is turning to a component of the lament psalm, in which prayer to God and openness to the future play key roles. His use of an affirmation of confidence hints that the time for dirgelike lamentation that takes only the past into account is over. Now the congregation needs to supplement its grief by turning to its God in prayer. A lament psalm will allow them to do both. The stage has been set for them to pray. We readers hope they have been listening and wonder how they will pray.

143

5

Fifth Poem (Lamentations 5)

The Congregation's Prayer as Turning Point

Here the goal of the previous poems is realized. In the third poem, the service leader called on the congregation to pray a prayer of repentance (lines 40–51). The fifth poem is that "lifting up of 'hearts and hands' to God in heaven" (Johnson 1985, 73) that he had urged. His call in the third poem put in plain language his earlier call to Zion to pray, in the second poem at stanzas 18 and 19, to which she responded with her prayer in stanzas 20–22. By so doing she functioned as a model for the members of the community, acting out an appropriate response they themselves should make to the tragedy of 586 BCE, including a response of prayer. Already in the first poem Zion had pointed the way forward by the role play of her urgent cries to God at the close of stanzas 9 and 11 and by her prayer in stanzas 20–22, while at the beginning and end of the third poem the mentor had encouragingly testified to his own prayers. So "the book as a whole . . . builds up towards the prayer of chapter 5" (Hunter 1996, 61).

Psychological closure for the community remains outside the range of this set of poems. It lay much further ahead and could not yet be achieved, so traumatic were the experiences they had undergone and were still undergoing. The modern preoccupation with closure impatiently rushes the sufferer to a premature conclusion. Closure must be allowed to take its own time. It is marked by eventual acceptance that is able to integrate previous suffering into one's life. However, there is still a rawness about the suffering of the fifth poem. Fresh wounds have brought their own resented pain. The poem cannot write a closed chapter on grief. Here is a lesser, but necessary, intermediate goal, to make contact with the God of Israel as a foundation for eventually rebuilding a life beyond devastating grief. Initiating such prayer was not an easy step for the shattered group to take, but, taking to heart the promptings in the earlier poems, the congregation managed to do so, presumably via its own representative(s). Their verbal participation is significant in itself, since, as has been said of grieving widows, "until they can talk, they have not really started on the road to recovery" (Caine 1974, 140). "No pain is so devastating as the pain a person refuses to face, and no suffering is so lasting as suffering left unacknowledged" (Gravitz and Bowden 1987, 37).

So this articulation marks a turning point within grief, the first sign of a positive movement beyond suffering in silence and toward eventual coping. It is a response to the call for a turning point that Berges has recognized in the second poem, *Get up* in stanza 19. The book of Lamentations refers to three such milestones encountered in the human experience of suffering. The first two lie outside the congregation's experience and are features of the mentor's testimonies in the third poem. In lines 21–24 he testified to a light bulb going off in his mind. He realized that, sufferer though he was, he was a survivor, thank God. Then in line 57 he recalled another time when he was given a message that his previous prayer for help would be answered, though it did not mean his crisis was over.

146

A turning point represents a new stage, a long-awaited readiness to start to move forward in some respect. C. S. Lewis wrote the final chapter of his chronicle of grief after reaching not closure but a turning point that was both gradual and sudden, already going on when first noticed, like the coming of daylight. It was a mixed experience. On the one hand, he was feeling a fresh stage of pain from the "amputation" of his loss. On the other hand, he found himself envisioning a more positive future (1976, 71, 75). Anne Brooks reached a similar point after her bereavement: "Most of the time I really am not fine, but not so bad . . . although the pain, when it comes, is still as intense" (1985, 30). And Francis Bridger testified about his turning point: "This is not the end. It is not the beginning of the end. But it is the end of the beginning" (2004, 112). Catherine Sanders (1999, 87–102), assessing the turning point in the grief process, describes it more as a transitional beginning, the taking of an initiative that moves beyond withdrawal. Here the still-suffering community is at last able to pray for a change for the better. To be exact, the poem itself is not the turning point but evidence of a turning point, which was a cognitive siding with the mentor and with Zion, a commitment to their joint perspective.

Gerstenberger is surely correct in hearing the community's vocal response in the *we* of this poem. The mentoring *we* spoken by the service leader in the third poem (lines 40–48) has been left behind, and so has his inclusive, narrating *we* in the fourth poem (stanzas 17–20). Now a new voice is heard. The way the series of poems has been developing indicates that at this point the congregation responds with its input to the promptings, direct and indirect, in the previous poems. Detailed examination will show how this prayer picks up their language and perspectives in compliance with Zion's modeling and the service leader's mentoring.

Yet there are three differences that show that this fifth poem develops in turn beyond its predecessors. First, the brevity of the poem, just twenty-two lines, is an indication of literary closure, concluding the shortening trend started in the fourth poem (Dobbs-Allsopp 1997, 59). Second, the alphabetic acrostic style that ran through the four earlier poems is now dropped. Only the twenty-two lines are left, as a reminiscence of the number of letters in the Hebrew alphabet; now each line is numbered, as in the third poem. The lack of an acrostic accompanies a radical shift in this last poem, while the number of lines is a token of continuity. The genre factor does not provide a reason for the dropping of the acrostic. Psalm 25, a lament psalm, has it. But in this case its as-sociation with pervasive grief in the earlier poems was presumably a consideration. Its absence symbolizes an ending of total grief and an embrace of hope. A door to the future now stands ajar.

Third, the meter of the Hebrew poetry is changed. The poem says good-bye to the limping meter of the dirge, three beats plus two beats, which pervades the earlier poems, and opts for a regular three-plus-three meter, apart from a few lines. The change fits the fact that the all-too-human dirge, which had eyes only for past sorrow and none for God or for any hope for the future, has been scrapped in favor of the format of the lament psalm. The lament psalm is a prayer to God and envisions a potential of renewal and restoration. It has necessarily taken a long time for the congregation to reach this point. The dirge style served them well by permitting full exploration of their grief as they listened to their fellow sufferer articulating their and his emotional and mental suffering and to Zion doing the same. It enabled them to own their catastrophic experience and let the horror of it all sink in. The new format, the lament psalm, still gives them room to ventilate their grief. But in this context it enables them to take to heart the testifying preaching of the third poem by tentatively venturing into new territory of hope.

The poem has its own momentum, inspired by communal laments in the Psalms, a threefold momentum of an initial petition offered to Yahweh, a grieving description of the community's troubles, and then closing petitions, both direct and indirect. The literary structure of the poem is often understood in terms of its arrangement of pronouns. The communal *we* in lines 1–10 switches to a focus on various groups in the community in lines 11–14 and then returns to *we* in lines 15–18 until a divine *you* joins it and comes to the fore in lines 19–22. However, Nägelsbach and Keil pointed to the refrain-like references to sinning in lines 7 and 16 as a clue to three sections, lines 1–7, 8–16, and 17–22. What makes their divisions impressive is that the poem then follows a pattern of strategic positioning encountered earlier. Weiser has compared the fourth poem, which used the technique of closing each of its four grief-laden sections with a short expression of guilt-related divine intervention. It is reasonable to assume that the congregation wants to continue a trend taught by their mentor by capping descriptions of grief with guilt-confessing refrains that transcend their brevity with a climactic quality.

Present Distress and Confession (5:1–7)

We readers are used to grieving descriptions of the community's anguish, but we need to appreciate in this case two changes from what we have read earlier. First, the service leader has mainly been sharing with the listening congregation the depth and breadth of their pain. It has been a way of working through that pain by bringing it to the surface of their conscious minds and facing its reality as it was talked through. The exceptions have been the instances where their suffering was brought not just to the congregation but to God in prayer, in the role modeling of Zion and of the service leader, a fellow sufferer. It has taken a long time, but now the community is ready to take over for itself those modeling, prayer-centered efforts. The descriptions of distress in this section and the next one are set in a prayer context. They fill out the pair of petitions in the first line addressed to God and so all function as prayer.

149

There is a second difference between this description and the previous ones. The accounts of the community's suffering in the previous poems have predominantly consisted of flashbacks that have relived the terrible period of the siege and, in the fourth poem, the traumatic fall of Jerusalem and its immediate aftermath. Those ghostly memories from the past haunted the community and preoccupied it. Rehearsing such nightmarish scenes in plain words was a necessary part of bringing a measure of relief to the troubled souls of the congregation. They were evidently able to take to heart the service leader's and Zion's grieving over the past and make it their own. Now they could move to the present, which the third poem had broached in its twelfth stanza (lines 34–36), to the lesser, but starkly real, problems of the foreign occupation of Judah that grievously threatened them on a daily basis. Life was still a bitter struggle that exposed them as vulnerable and powerless.

> [1]Call to mind, Yahweh, what has happened to us.
>> Take notice and look at our contemptible state.
> [2]Our ancestral property has been turned over to aliens,
>> our homes to foreigners.
> [3]We have become orphans, fatherless;
>> our mothers are virtual widows.
> [4]We must pay to drink our own water;
>> our own wood comes at a price.
> [5]We have taskmasters who breathe down our necks;
>> we get exhausted, but are permitted no rest.
> [6]To Egypt we offered the hand of submission,
>> to Assyria too, to get enough bread.
> [7]Our forebears who sinned are here no more;
>> we are the ones bearing the punishment of their wrongs.

The initial petitions are cries for help, like those of a stranded motorist waving down a passing car. "Stop what you are doing, Yahweh," they plead. "Give us your full attention and put our plight on your agenda." Similarly, the psalmist prays, "Look upon my suffering and deliver me" (Ps. 119:153). The community's appeal to *take notice and look* responds to cues from Zion's brief outburst in the first poem at the end of stanza 11, *Look, Yahweh, and take notice how despicable I have become*, and from her introductory *Look, Yahweh, and take notice* in the prayer she prays at the close of the second poem. The service leader had testified to his own petition, *Take notice of [my enemies]* at the end of the third poem, at line 63. The congregation shows it has been listening. They now echo the role modeling of Zion and of their mentor. In the first and third cases, the petitions earlier in the book had been accompanied by a strong feeling of grievance over suffering at the hands of human enemies, and the same will prove to be the case here. The congregation acts on the permission it has been given to express its own sense of grievance rather than simply adopting the model communal prayer in the third poem (lines 42–47) that focused on repentance without grievance.

Warrant for importing its particular grievance into the prayer comes from earlier in the third poem, the preacher's assurance in lines 34–36 that *the Lord looks at* the offenses against human rights perpetrated by the postwar occupying forces. The congregation suffering from the occupation turns this assurance into its own prayer, while incorporating expressions of repentance. The initial verb *call to mind* will eventually be rephrased with a sharper edge to it in line 20—with a charge that God had ignored and neglected their cause—but there is no such nuance here. They make their respectful request to God, hoping for the divine consideration, compassion, and commitment that the community needs. The grievance they bring is their bad treatment from others, in the hope of triggering a positive response, namely that, in New Testament terms, "he will quickly grant justice to them" (Luke 18:8).

The long stretch of material in the first two sections is an exposition of the community's experience, their *contemptible state* in the initial line. It is much longer than the description of distress that customarily appears in psalm laments, but it appropriately fits the pattern of lengthy, dirgelike descriptions that had occurred in the earlier poems. The community's plight demanded, they felt, no less an outpouring of deep grief, and they welcome the implicit encouragement of their mentor to speak at length. They give a report to God about the postwar occupation of Judah—both the capital and other towns will be mentioned in the same breath in line 11. A litany of protests is laid out in lines 2–5 about the harsh regime that had taken over their lives.

First, they had lost their homes, which the occupying forces had requisitioned. It is a heartrending hardship that war tends to bring in its train, suffered for instance by the Poles when Russia invaded the eastern half of their country in 1939. In Israelite culture, however, it was a particularly crushing blow. It clashed with the tradition of land tenure by which real estate passed from genera-tion to generation in the same family. The tradition had a strong theological foundation because the land was regarded as Yahweh's perennial gift, distributed among tribes, clans, and families. The line lacks the blatancy of Psalm 79:1, "O God, the nations have invaded *your* inheritance," but the situation is charged with divine associations. Yahweh had a stake in the people's victimization. They had a common cause against a mutual enemy.

Mention of orphans and widows looks at first glance like a refer-ence to family losses from male bereavement or even exile. However, the simile in the second half of line 3 (NIV, "like widows") signals to readers that the first half is meant as a metaphor. Widows and orphans stand here not for groups within the community but for the community itself plunged into insecurity. There is an echo of Zion's widow-like plight in stanza 1 of the first poem. The congregation felt unprotected and helpless, prey to disorienting troubles they had never known before, in normal times. The admission carries with it an implicit appeal. Hosea 14:3 makes it more explicitly, where Israel was urged to affirm to God that "in you the fatherless find compassion." Psalm 10:4 makes a similar appeal to God in declaring that "you are the helper of the fatherless."

Lines 4 and 5 state factual grievances. Water and firewood were no longer commodities for anyone to use free of charge. The occupying authorities treated such natural resources as their own property to exploit by taxation. They usurped the people's right to have free access to them. This is another manifestation of the initial protest in line 2. There are latent echoes of a God-given land blessed with resources for the people to enjoy (cf. Deut. 8:7–10; 11:11–12; contrast Deut. 2:6, 28). This was a wrong turn of events; it marked the loss of a significant civil freedom. Line 5 deplores the rigor of forced labor and in particular the time demands that came with it. In intensity and in duration the work they had to do was too much. They were being worn down, never able to rest and recoup their strength. As Boecker comments, this was a terrible imposition on a community used to a weekly Sabbath rest.

In the closing pair of lines, the section goes off at a double tangent. It veers from the present to the past and from grief-laden appeal and grievance to confession. Ending on this latter note is nothing new but picks up a cue from the fourth poem. The connection of line 6 with the context is the restricted availability of basic resources. The community's access not only to water and wood but also to bread was adversely affected, as line 9 will testify. Yet in stating that bread was in short supply, the community recalled they were standing shoulder to shoulder with earlier generations. And what had those generations done? They had gone cap in hand to foreign powers, signing away their national independence in economic treaties. No wonder the present generation was in a similar, but worse, plight now! After the camels of Egypt and Assyria had been invited into Judah's tent, it should be no surprise that a new camel, Babylon, had taken it over. From another metaphorical perspective, what Judah had sown earlier it was reaping now.

It is tempting, but misguided, to relate this backward look to the exiles' petulant cry in Ezekiel 18:2, echoed in Jeremiah 31:29, "The fathers eat sour grapes, and the children's teeth are set on edge." To change the imagery, their predecessors had done the drinking and they had gotten the hangover. Here, however, the sectional parallel, *we sinned*, in line 16 points to an affirmation of responsibility rather than a denial, which would run counter to the tenor of the book. Likewise in Psalm 79 "the sins of the fathers" (v. 8) are paired with "our sins" (v. 9), while Psalm 106:6 confesses, "We have sinned, even as our fathers did." Similarly, Jeremiah 22:21 traces Jerusalem's disobedience continuously back to its early history, "from your youth." Here the community is confessing the generational solidarity involved in its sinning. The inclusive *we* in line 6 says as much, as Kraus and Brandscheidt (1983, 197) have observed.

The divine punishment perceived not only in the siege and capture of Jerusalem but also in the occupation that followed was an eventual crackdown on a longstanding issue. If Judah pursued a policy of economic dependence on foreigners, so be it! The collective punishment ironically fit the crime. Readers may recall the simple story of Joseph's brothers' journeying to Egypt to buy grain (Gen. 42:1–5). Here, however, there is a sinister edge to such visits, taken over from the preexilic prophets. Earlier in the book, especially in the second poem, correspondence with prophetic teaching was noticeable. The part of that teaching that is relevant here was an outcry against political alliances with the great powers as inconsistent with traditional faith in Yahweh. It is illustrated, for instance, in Isaiah 30:1–7 and Jeremiah 2:18–19, 36. The community adds its amen to that prophetic perspective. The grounds of such alliances are generally presented as military; here they are plausibly described as driven by economic needs. "As a people they have a history of disloyalty to God" (Bergant 2003, 129).

Humiliation, Sorrow, and Confession (5:8–16)

The second section of the poem speaks twice about the harassment the community had to endure during the postwar occupation and of its grim effects on their lives, in lines 8 and 9–10 and again in 11–14 and 15–16, before a final confession of guilt in the closing half-line. In the second part, lines 11–14 expand on the arbitrary lawlessness of line 8, which is accordingly a headline for the section; the repetition of *their hands* in line 12 so suggests. Once more grievance and grief are combined and then compounded with guilt.

> [8]Underlings are in control of us;
>> there is nobody to rescue us from their hands.
> [9]We risk our lives to get the bread we need,
>> threatened by the sword in the wilderness.
> [10]Our skin is burning as if in an oven
>> from the fever caused by hunger.
> [11]They have sexually assaulted women in Zion,
>> as well as girls in Judah's towns.
> [12]They have used their hands to hang up royal
>> officials;
>> elders are shown no honor.
> [13]Young men have to wield the grinding millstones
>> and boys stagger as they haul the wood.
> [14]Old men have left the city gate,
>> young men their music playing.
> [15]Our hearts have lost their joy,
>> our dancing has changed to mourning;
> [16]garlands have fallen off our heads—
>> what a tragedy for us that we sinned!

The community members, conscious of the indignities that had been heaped upon them, voiced before God their litany of grievances. The occupying forces lacked any sense of moral responsibility in their management of the occupied territory of Judah. Minor officials swaggered around, giving orders that must be obeyed and taking liberties that could not be refused. The community resented their despotic and arbitrary exercise of power. How were lives affected? They were put at serious risk, as citizens ventured into the countryside to harvest the barley and wheat crops growing on their smallholdings. In the context of occupation, *the sword in the wilderness* is best understood as a reference to detachments of troops who thought nothing of attacking the families farming in the fields as a diversion on their march to the next town. In the book of Jeremiah the sword typically refers to Babylonian military attack. In a chain of dire consequences this agricultural hazard discouraged harvesting, which caused scarcity of food, which led to lowering of immunity and so ill health, especially an outbreak of fever.

What were the particular indignities carried out by the *hands* of the occupying forces in the cities? No social class was immune from their wanton behavior. They had no respect for the Judean womenfolk, young and old, in Jerusalem or other towns, treating them as sexual objects to satisfy their lust. They took delight in singling out adult men who had held responsible positions in the Judean community, *royal officials* and *elders*, publicly hoisting the former as a hazing spectacle, in ridicule of their high status, and deliberately humiliating the latter. Young males were put to forced labor, the daily chore of grinding the grain that women convention-ally did (Eccles. 12:3; Luke 17:35), and to grueling work beyond their physical capacity. The public squares stood unnaturally empty and silent. No more could *old men* be seen meeting there and chatting out of the sun on seats inside the gate structures (cf. Ruth 4:1), while no *young men* could be heard making music.

This grim experience of occupation had plunged the whole community into deep, unnatural gloom. Total sadness prevailed, where once joy and conviviality had been commonplace. But grief and grievance were not adequate responses unless room was made for guilt. By way of climax the members of the congregation own up to the root cause of their social degradation. They bring their own amen to the service leader's mentoring and to Zion's role modeling, which had earlier affirmed the fulfillment of the preexilic prophets' denunciations of the community's sinning. They plead guilty with their prayer of confession, as the climax of the section, and take full responsibility for the plight in which they find themselves. Along with line 7, it is their heartfelt apology to God.

Challenging Cries for Help (5:17–22)

> [17]Here is why we have become sick at heart,
> the reason why we are bleary-eyed:
> [18]The reason is Mount Zion that lies devastated,
> the haunt of jackals.
> [19]As for you, Yahweh, you sit enthroned forever,
> your throne continues generation after
> generation.
> [20]Why is it you constantly ignore us,
> neglect us for so long?
> [21]"Bring us back" to yourself, Yahweh, "so we can
> come back."
> Renew our lives like they were before—
> [22]but you have rejected us outright
> and are angry with us to an extreme degree!

In the closing section, the community draws on a prayer tradition found among the lament psalms of the book of Psalms, a tradition of complaining to God in aggrieved tones. One third of the lament psalms are made up of complaints that protest against God. "The aim of these psalms, however, is never simply to complain, for this protest is always directed toward the purpose of summoning God to conform to his promises" (Broyles 1989, 221). Such complaints also confront God with rhetorical questions: Why? How long? These questions maintain that there is something terribly wrong in the present situation. They claim it is God's responsibility to acknowledge this truth and to intervene appropriately. In particular, they challenge God to live up to the praise traditionally brought in Israel's hymns. The complaints are subdivided into two groups, one that complains about divine absence and neglect, and another that protests divinely caused suffering (Morrow 2006, 57–60). The close of the fifth poem aligns with the former group, examples of which are Psalms 13; 22; 35; and 42–43.

These complaints run counter to Christian norms of prayer, but they do have a few New Testament counterparts (Morrow 2006, 174). In Mark's account of the stilling of the storm, the disciples utter a cry to the sleeping Jesus not found in Matthew's or Luke's narratives: "Teacher, don't you care if we drown?" (Mark 4:38; cf. Ps. 44:23–24). Their protest expresses a bewildered sense of grave inconsistency between the Jesus they knew and the way he was now behaving. And in Revelation 6:10 the souls of martyred believers bring their complaint to God: "How long, Sovereign Lord, holy and true, until you . . . avenge our blood?" They are told to wait a little longer. Eventually their complaint is vindicated, and so a great multitude in heaven glorifies God: "He has avenged the blood of his servants" (Rev. 19:2). Elie Wiesel has wisely written that "Abraham and Moses, Jeremiah and Rebbe Levi-Yitzhak of Berdichev teach us that it is permissible for man to accuse God, provided that it be done in the name of faith in God" (1995, 84). Likewise Claus Westermann has affirmed about those who complain: "The sufferers continue to cling to God, whom they no longer understand" (1998, 239).

The heart of this complaint or expression of grievance against God is the praise that appears in line 19 about Yahweh's role as king, permanently enthroned. In the psalms it is praise such as one would find in a hymn, where the reader is meant to take it at face value. In a complaint psalm, however, its function is "to show Yahweh the contradictory nature of his present behavior, and to remind him of what his conduct should be" (Broyles 1989, 44). In fact, the main title of Broyles's book, *The Conflict of Faith and*

Experience in the Psalms, sums up the dilemma that underlies the complaint. Faith points in one direction, and experience the other way. Whereas the fourth poem bemoaned the shattering of fundamental beliefs on which the community's existence had been based, here one of those beliefs, an aspect of Zion theology, is not abandoned but reclaimed and fought for in God's hearing. Did the expression of hope for *Lady Zion* at the close of the previous poem promote the claim? At this time the temple mount, *Mount Zion*, lay in ruins. The congregation's members maintain this to be the prime source of their grief—and tacitly urge that it should be a deep concern to Yahweh also since in Israelite tradition the temple was a monument to Yahweh's everlasting kingship. Their God was "the King of glory" who had entered the temple gates (Ps. 24:7–10). *Mount Zion* was "the mountain where God chooses to reign, where the LORD himself will dwell forever" (Ps. 68:16). The comparison between the building of God's "sanctuary" and "the high heavens" and "the earth, which he founded forever" in Psalm 78:69 (NRSV) implies that the temple reflected the heavenly palace and was to be everlasting.

This glorious truth is the basis for the bewildered question in line 20: *Why is it you constantly ignore us, neglect us for so long?* In the light of temple-linked divine kingship, the ruined temple was a contradiction in terms. It also mirrored Yahweh's equally anomalous outright rejection of the covenant people. Psalm 74 runs on similar lines. There the petitions, "Remember Mount Zion, where you came to dwell. Direct your steps to the perpetual ruins" (vv. 2–3 NRSV), are justification for the previous question, "Why have you rejected us forever, O God?" (v. 1). Here in Lamentations 5, praise of Yahweh's everlasting kingship is cited as incompatible with the present situation. Listen to a modern example of using praise as a challenge. It comes from an account of a young Austrian girl who in 1938 was uprooted from her orthodox Jewish home in Vienna and taken to England with other children to escape from the Nazis.

A Hanukkah service was arranged for the young refugees. "There was a certain amount of desperation in our singing," she recalled. "As if by shouting *Ma'oz Tzur* [a Hanukkah hymn] loud enough and with enough fervor, we might reach God on his throne, knock him off his pedestal, and get him to come down and put everything to rights again" (Korobkin 2008, 103).

"Why?" in the complaint psalms is never an intellectual request for information but a loaded rhetorical question that conveys emotional bewilderment and protest. It expresses an indirect petition that God should act otherwise, to be consistent with the divine character. Modern grief accounts are full of questions that begin with "Why?" No doubt some readers can recall their own. I will never forget the day when at the age of eleven I was home from school, sick with flu, and my older sister came into my bedroom to tell me our mother in the next room had just died of a heart attack. When she had gone to phone the doctor, I thumped my pillow as hard as I could and said aloud, "Why did you have to let her die, God?" Ann Weems poses this type of question in much of her grieving poetry, such as "Where were you? / Why didn't you stop it?" "You are the power: / Why didn't you use it?" and "Why didn't you let me be there / for him?" (1995, 15, 20, 101).

Usually such questions are dirgelike, relating solely to an unchangeable past. Martha and Mary's complaining statements to Jesus about his delay in responding to their message of their brother's illness (John 11:21, 32) were like that. In the complaint psalms, however, the questions characteristically refer to a present crisis and urge God to change it on behalf of those who pray— "for your name's sake," one might say. "The complaints . . . are appeals in order to bring about change" (Westermann 1998, 239). Weems honors this usage by sometimes framing her questions in this way: "Why are you ignoring me?" "Why can't I walk with you / in peace once more?" "Why don't you protect me / against my emotions?" (1995, 32, 64, 86). Her first question—"Why are you ignoring me?"—coincides with our text at line 20: *Why is it you constantly ignore us?* The similarity is a hint that such a complaint can have a legitimate place in contemporary Christian praying.

Here two issues are addressed: the absence of God from the scene and the duration of such absence. The former issue reminds readers of the opening of Psalm 22, whose first half expresses complaint: "My God, my God, why have you forsaken me? Why are you so far from saving me, from the words of my groaning?" There too duration was a factor: "O my God, I cry out by day, but you do not answer, by night, and am not silent." Such questions function as indirect petitions for God to act otherwise. In this case the question is a stronger version of the petition, *Call to mind what has happened to us*, in line 1. As yet, there had been no indications of God's active intervention to help or bless. Instead, the community sensed they stood alone, the bereft orphans and widows of line 3, no longer treated as members of God's family. The prolonging of their suffering made the situation worse: *Why neglect us for so long?* This problem echoes the question "How long?" found in complaint psalms (e.g., Pss. 13:2; 74:10; 89:46). "Enough already!" is the congregation's virtual cry. It is a cry that will eventually receive a prophet's answer in Isaiah 40:2, in the assurances that Jerusalem's "hard service has been completed, that her sin has been paid for, that she has received from the LORD's hand double"—already more than enough—"for all her sins." But such answers lay in the future. For now the community could only pray and wait.

In line 21, the congregation utters two direct petitions that match the pair at the beginning of the poem. They pray for the gap they perceive between them and Yahweh to be bridged from the divine side. The God they had known was conspicuously absent from their midst. No evidence of the positive divine presence they had once enjoyed could be seen in the *contemptible state* of line 1, which had overwhelmed them. They had done all they could in appealing to God and confessing their sinfulness in repentance. But was God willing to accept their prayers? The onus was now on God to be prepared to take them back into the spiritual relationship that had once bonded them both. The contrast with Yahweh's ignoring and rejecting them in the lines before and after shows that this is the meaning. Boecker so observes, comparing Romans 9:16, "So it depends not on human will or exertion, but on God who shows mercy" (NRSV). If, and only if, Yahweh took them back, the opportunity would come for the community's rehabilitation, for them to regain the divine blessings of normal living they had earlier enjoyed. There is a harking back to the nostalgia for the way things used to be, in the first poem (stanza 7). When, however, normal living came, it would be a new normal rather than the old one they expected.

In the third poem at line 40, the preacher had urged the congregation to *come back to Yahweh* with a prayer of repentance. But, even as they did so, the question remained open, whether they would get spiritual reinstatement, and for this they now plead. In the first half of the line *Bring us back, so we can come back* seems to be a quotation from Jeremiah 31:18 (Berges). It changes singular pronouns to plural and adds *to yourself* to make the meaning clear. That text originally narrated a yearning for spiritual reconciliation on the part of northerners ("Ephraim"), who were left in the land after the fall of Samaria in 721 BCE. Now history had virtually repeated itself. Southerners found themselves in a similar situation, and they borrowed the petition. Perhaps its sequel was also in the congregation's minds, God's assurance that "my heart yearns for him [Ephraim]; I have great compassion for him" (Jer. 31:20).

The alternative was a ghastly one. What if Yahweh's anger had not yet played itself out and they were doomed to have the relationship with their God permanently severed? The congregation deplores that possibility. At first sight the presence of line 22 is a surprise on stylistic grounds because line 21 would make a fine ending, with its pair of petitions forming a neat frame with those in line 1. Yet from a broader stylistic perspective, a twenty-second line is to be expected since it aligns with the numerical patterning of the four earlier poems. So it must have a deliberate role here. What that role is can be determined by comparing an element that is found in complaint psalms. The issue of anger and/or rejection, permanent or not, is raised regularly in such psalms. It can take the form of questions: "How long, O LORD? Will you be angry forever?" (Ps. 79:5) and "Why have you rejected us forever, O God? Why does your anger smolder against the sheep of your pasture?" (Ps. 74:1). Or it can be a direct negative appeal: "Do not reject us forever" (Ps. 44:23). The issue of angry rejection can also be phrased as a statement, like line 22 here: "You have rejected us, O God, . . . you have been angry—now restore us" (Ps. 60:1) and "But you have rejected, you have spurned, you have been very angry with your anointed one" (Ps. 89:38).

A statement format occurs in line 22. In fact, lines 19 and 21–22 mirror on a smaller scale the development in Psalm 89. There it is claimed that God's immense power over the world and solemn promise to maintain the Davidic covenant, celebrated in verses 1–37, are belied by the impending end of the monarchy and by Yahweh's not lifting a finger to help. Here there is a similar movement from praise to challenging statement. There the appeals to God to remember and so intervene occur later, in verses 47 and 50. Here they occur in the middle, in the form of the questions of line 20, which are indirect petitions for God not to ignore or neglect the people. In this case the statement of rejection is left until the very end, for maximum effectiveness.

What is the function of the issue of severe anger and/or rejection that is raised in the complaint psalms? Raising the issue there is meant to invite a reassurance from God that such is not or will not be the case. Broyles, discussing the more common question format, says, "This type of question, by pushing God to the extremes, constrains him to answer with 'No!'" (1989, 82). The same is clearly true of the statement format, as the case in Psalm 60:1 shows. In line with this expectation of a divine turnabout, Psalm 85 follows up the question "Will you be angry with us forever?" (v. 5) with a more reasonable proposal, "Will you not revive us again, that your people may rejoice in you?" (v. 6). Then an oracular promise is given that denies the people's foreboding by affirming their desire (vv. 8–13). Far from being angry forever, God would show favor. Similarly, in Isaiah 49:14–16, Zion's statement that Yahweh has abandoned and forgotten her is followed by a compassionate denial. Within this section of the fifth poem, especially since it is so closely modeled on the complaint psalms, it is surely correct to see the same intention in the statement of line 22, the intention to coax a positive response from God.

When this passage is read out in the synagogue, it is traditional to repeat line 21 at the end, to leave the congregation with those positive petitions ringing in their ears, instead of the alternative of line 22, one too terrible to dwell on. But that misses the point—to function as a sting in the tail. Repeating the line takes a new audience into account and spells the virtual displacement of the intended hearer, God. The purpose of placing line 22 at the end was the hope that so extreme a conclusion would force a denial on God's part by intervening on the side of the oppressed in a positive fashion. "It is a 'ploy' of the suppliant, to cause Yahweh to face up to His covenant obligations" (Heater 1992, 313). The praying congregation waits for God to answer and to act. The closing line does not cancel their prayer for restoration. It does not deny their rekindled belief in Yahweh's everlasting kingship and power. It does affirm the enormous gap God has put between them, a gap glaringly symbolized by the temple ruins. It is now up to Yahweh to close that otherwise permanent gap and to act like the father in Luke 15:20 who, seeing his prodigal and repentant son still a long way off and filled with compassion, ran toward him and embraced him.

What role does the closing section of complaint (lines 17–22) play in the contexts of the prayer as a whole and of the previous four poems? The first two sections of the prayer have been shown to respond to promptings supplied earlier by the service leader and by Zion, his pastoral helper. The last, complaint-laden section is a new kind of impassioned prayer that challenges God to help. At first sight it looks inconsistent with the earlier part of the prayer, which placed structural focus on the community's sinning, and so with the previous poems. As sinners (lines 7 and 16), surely they had no standing before God. In particular, the conclusion of the sermon in the third poem had asked, *Why should anyone protest about the punishment of his sins?* In fact, confession of sins does sometimes appear in complaint psalms in the book of Psalms. Psalm 79 admits to a history of sinning in verses 8–9 and yet hopes in verse 5 that Yahweh's reaction of anger will not last "forever." The divine punishment was thought to be excessive and threatening the extinction of God's people, and there is a plea for God to stop. Psalms 85, 89, and 90 make the same argument (Broyles 1989, 219–20).

Accordingly, in this case the congregation had no quarrel with its leader's prophetic interpretation of the fall of Jerusalem and the collapse of the state and its institutions as the negative work of God. It can all be accepted as evidence of the dire presence of God, in reprisal for the nation's wrongdoing. Now, during the postwar occupation, they envision Yahweh as manifesting a different kind of negativity, as absent and letting the enemies' oppression take its course. In the complaint psalms, divine rejection and anger can be associated either with God's hostile presence (Ps. 60:1–3) or absence (Ps. 74:1, 11) (Broyles 1989, 62–63). Here the congregation can still see some justice in this divine absence. But does it mean that God has said a final farewell? Surely not. They grapple with the tension between the God they had known through their theological traditions and the negative evidence of God they have perceived in their recent history and present experience. They yearn for the spiritual relationship to be restored. "Restore us, O God," they virtually ask; "make your face shine upon us, that we may be saved" (Ps. 80:3). "We have suffered enough," they plead. "Can't we start over now?"

This is not a voice of defiance, though it does take a stand over against God. The congregation had listened with absolute seriousness to the service leader's theological arguments laid before them in the sermon of the third poem, as an incentive for their praying. He had argued that divine compassion follows suffering, that divine grace prevails, and so that *the Lord's rejection does not last forever* (lines 31–32). Accordingly, they had come to accept that "though our pain is true, it is not the absolute truth" (Newlin 2006, 130). The congregation's complaint of divine rejection stays within the bounds of faith because it accompanies their stand on the traditional promises of God reaffirmed by their leader. Even the sentiment "Enough already!" is far from being impertinent. It gets its pertinence from the leader's assurance given to Zion, *he will keep you in exile no longer*, at the close of the fourth poem. The congregation stands up for the reality and relevance of God despite all appearances.

It is important to grasp that the complaint tradition used at the climax of this final poem is born of extremity and desperation. When believers find themselves in such a fearfully dark valley, the biblical tradition is there, providing challenging words for souls in pain to use. Rosemary was such a soul. She was an intelligent and devout patient in her early twenties. Evidently she had a physical ailment that at irregular intervals broke savagely into her life and made it unpredictable and stressful. She had come into the hospital for a series of tests, which she hoped would lead to a straightforward surgical procedure and a new, healthy life. In her ailment she lacked comforters. Her father had died, and her mother had gone on to marry a loving man and move out of state. She had an older brother who lived contentedly in a city far to the north with his wife and child. She felt horribly alone, isolated from the happy members of her family upon whom she did not want to intrude with her troubles. I paid her a number of visits, getting to know her stories and praying with her about the tests. One afternoon I found her distraught. That morning her doctor had bluntly told her he could not operate. There was no physiological basis for her symptoms, he said, and her illness was psychological in origin. In her mind, she heard him accusing her of imagining things. It was the last straw. She turned angrily against God for making her suffer so much. I listened and then asked, "May I read you a psalm?" I read Psalm 88, a complaint psalm that cries out bitterly for help to "the God of my salvation" (Ps. 88:1 NRSV). As I read, she was able to hear her own feelings, spoken from a place within the circle of faith. At the end she said, "I didn't know words like that were in the Bible. What was the number of that psalm? I'd like to read it in my Bible after you've gone."

A couple of years later I encountered her on a psychiatric ward of the hospital. Nothing serious. She was having her medication checked. She had chummed up with another girl, and together they brightened the ward. She was coping and moving on with her life. At one point in her life her best medicine had been a psalm of complaint. It enabled her to sort out her frightened emotions and to find a place for them inside the bounds of faith. Sometimes the most appropriate spirituality for the believer is what has been called a "spirituality of protest" (Brueggemann in Weems 1995, xii).

The first two sections of the prayer make further room for the grief, grievance, and guilt that preoccupied the earlier poems because that was how the particular suffering in view needed to be expressed. Now it has all been laid before God. Readers have heard the grief throbbing throughout the prayer in the tale of the occupation and coming to a head in lines 15 and 16. Grievance against the occupying forces has been keenly voiced, but in this case relief rather than reprisal has been sought. Guilt has provided a refrain for the prayer's first two sections and so motivated the closing petition for the spiritual restoration of God's prodigal family. The congregation has taken at least two of the steps prescribed for the recovering alcoholic by Alcoholics Anonymous. Step 2, "Came to believe that a Power greater than ourselves could restore us to sanity," which comes on the heels of human powerlessness expressed in step 1, is reflected in the turning to God in the prayer of the fifth poem. And step 7, "Humbly asked Him to remove our shortcomings," which expresses the owning of personal responsibility that lies at the heart of AA, finds parallels in the congregation's acute awareness of the sinning that had broken their earlier relationship with God and, finally, in their longing for spiritual restoration that alone could spell newness of life.

In the last section of the prayer, Israel's own prayer tradition permitted them to bring a complaint that forcibly expresses the congregation's other grievance, against God. The emotional energy that had earlier in the book demanded reprisal against human foes is now channeled instead into a new grievance, against God. This is not only an Old Testament phenomenon. In Luke 18:1–8, Jesus tells a parable that embraces a double grievance, human and divine. The parable of the unjust judge encourages the disciples to "cry out to God day and night" in a nagging sort of way until they saw justice done against their oppressors. Similarly, the souls of Christian martyrs can shout their double complaint, "How long . . . until you judge the inhabitants of the world and avenge our blood?" (Rev. 6:10), and eventually get their answer.

The fifth poem of Lamentations attests a stage that has superseded the third poem in one respect. The congregation's members no longer need the warning not to be in denial about their guilt, given there in line 39. But the rest of the third poem remains valid, providing among other things a theological basis for the fifth in its message of grace after suffering and its corollary to wait in hope.

And that is one way to apply the story of Jesus's stilling the storm in Mark 4:35–41.

When Raymond, the young man whose story of inconsolable grief was related in the introduction to this book, awoke from his much-needed sleep, he may not have recalled my visit. Exhaustion and depression are powerful soporifics. Yet, I suspect, those three words—tears, talk, time—fell like seeds into his unconscious and germinated in the weeks that followed. The mourning of his personal tragedy would not have a quick or easy closure, but hope emerges from mourning. Hope, the instrument of healing, has very small seeds, but they are life-giving. Believing individuals, caught up in a turmoil of suffering and grieving, from those in the Lamentations congregation down to us who suffer and those who care for us, are bidden to wait in hope. Part of that waiting may even be to challenge a Lord whom they perceive to be uncaringly asleep or, in C. S. Lewis's forthright words, "so very absent a help in time of trouble" (1976, 5).

Notes on the Translation

The translation is the product of my own study. In citing other biblical books I have used the NIV, unless otherwise stated. In these notes I refer for comparison to a sample group of seven standard English versions: the NIV, NRSV, REB, NJPS, NAB, NJB, and GNT. There are occasional references to the KJV, RSV, and NEB. The notes also refer to ancient versions in Greek, Latin, Syriac, and Aramaic, which are witnesses to the basic Hebrew text. The earliest extant Greek version does not represent the early so-called Septuagint, though nearly all commentators wrongly so claim or imply. It features a later revision that may be tentatively dated about 50 BCE, which reflects the then-current Hebrew text (Barthélemy 1963, 33, 47, 158–60; Tov 2001, 145; Schäfer 2006, 238n1). Accordingly, the Greek version is not as valuable as in other books. The Qumran fragments of Lamentations, which Hillers usefully discusses, have not in my view yielded preferable readings.

> 1:2 *allies*: Compare "friends" in the NJPS and GNT. A number of the English versions render "lovers." As Brunet (1968, 6) observes, the Hebrew refers to a legitimate relationship, as in 1 Kings 5:1 (Hebrew 15), rather than a culpable one,

for which an intensive form would be expected, as for example in Ezek. 23:5, 9. Provan also cautions against this view.

1:3 *after*: This temporal sense of the preposition is adopted by the NIV and NJB, given as an option by Hillers, and favored by Provan and Berlin.

1:4 *feel devastated*: The verb is usually interpreted in terms of material ruin, but its use for personal emotion in 1:13, 16 and 3:11 and the present context of grief suggest that personification and grieving are in view here.

1:6 *majesty, royal officials*: For the royal character of the first term, compare Ps. 21:5 (Hebrew 6); for that of the second, compare Lam. 2:2, 9.

and so . . . hunter: The simile continues to the end of the stanza, as the NJB, REB, and GNT have judged, following Ehrlich (1914, 30).

1:7 *remembered*: A past tense, as Berlin renders, is preferable.

1:8 *an object of mockery*: The NRSV and NJPS render similarly.

1:10 The bizarre interpretation of this stanza in terms of a detailed description of the rape of the woman-city, found in Mintz (1982, 4) and adopted by Dobbs-Allsopp, Berlin, and O'Connor, is an imaginative imposition on the text that creates exegetical overload.

1:11 *their valuables*: Brandscheidt (1983, 116) rightly rejects Hillers's interpretation in terms of children as importing a novel note into the contextual concern for material valuables.

1:12 *Should . . . your concern*: The traditional interpretation, retained by the NRSV, NIV, and REB, can stand. Only tone of voice need indicate a question in the original. The Hebrew preposition is used in the sense of a similar one, to convey a duty or obligation resting upon someone.

1:14 *were tied*: The Hebrew verb occurs only here, but the context points to this meaning.

1:15 *army*: The NAB, NIV, and GNT render thus, while NJB has "host."

1:17 *Jacob's foes to surround it*: The REB, NJB, NJPS, and GNT construe in this way.

1:20 *Because of . . . defiance*: Nägelsbach and Rudolph rightly link this with the next line.

    outside . . . inside: The city is in view, as the NIV and NJB seem to imply, rather than outdoors and indoors. Jeremiah 14:18 is a good parallel text.

1:21 *Listen*: A singular imperative is reflected in the Syriac version and has been adopted in the NAB, NJB, and GNT. Reyburn and Renkema, both conservative textual critics, endorse this slight change in the Hebrew text as warranted by the context.

    May you bring: The NIV renders thus, rightly taking the verbal form as a precative use of the perfect, which the imperatives in other modern versions may also imply.

2:3 *their right hands*: literally "his right hand," referring to either Israel or Yahweh. The rest of the stanza refers to Yahweh's active opposition to Israel, which suggests the former option (Ehrlich 1914, 35; Hillers; Pham 1999, 103).

2:5 (also 7) *Zion's (fortified buildings)*: literally "her."
    Israel's (fortresses): literally "his."

2:6 *as if a garden hut*: The Hebrew word for *tabernacle* also means "hut, temporary structure." The construction is an abbreviated comparison, "as if (that of) a garden" (Ehrlich 1914, 36). Gottlieb (1978, 28–29) compares Gen. 18:11; Ps. 18:33 (Hebrew 34) for this construction. The NAB interprets in this way.

2:10 *old men*: Reyburn and the NAB and GNB so render, rather than "elders."

2:11 *bile*: The NRSV and REB so translate, while the NAB has "gall." Literally "liver," it has this meaning by metonymy.

    my poor people: The Hebrew personifying phrase, literally "daughter (of) my people," is used in prophetic texts in a lament context, for example in Isa. 22:4; Jer. 6:26 ("my poor people," NRSV), and seems to express compassion.

2:13 *analogy*: The context and the similar questions in Isa. 40:18, which Westermann compares, require such a meaning, perhaps from a basic sense of the Hebrew verb as "repeat" and so "present another case" (Albrektson 1963, 108).

2:14 *bland*: "Whitewash" (NJB), approved by some commentators with appeal to Ezek. 13:10–16, which refers metaphorically to a whitewashed wall, does not fit so well contextually. This adjective and the preceding one refer to a lack of positive qualities (Albrektson 1963, 110).

misleading: The NAB, NRSV, NIV, and a number of commentators so render.

2:18 *Call out*: An imperative is required in the light of the rest of the stanza and v. 19, and most modern versions so render. The Hebrew, which means "their hearts called out" and is reflected in the ancient versions, may have been a marginal comment clarifying that the address to Zion's wall is metaphorical and ultimately intended for humans to respond to sincerely (cf. 3:41). If so, the comment displaced the original text at an early stage (Gottlieb 1978, 37).

2:20 *On whom . . . this*: Ehrlich (1914, 38), Albrektson (1963, 19–20), and House so interpret, while the NAB, NJB, and NIV are similar.

when . . . when: Ehrlich (1914, 38) found subordinate clauses here. The extent of the divine affliction is illustrated in these clauses. The first two lines of v. 21 continue the illustration, while its third line and the first line of v. 22 revisit the affliction.

3:17 *had no room for*: The unusual Hebrew construction occurs elsewhere with similar verbs, "forget" in Ps. 102:4 (Hebrew 5) and "forsake" in Jer. 18:14.

3:19 *Pondering*: The verb is taken as an infinitive, here used as a verbal noun. Four of the sample English translations interpret in this way.

3:22 *have not ended*: The Aramaic and the Syriac versions reflect this reading, which provides the expected parallelism between the two half-lines. Unfortunately, the Greek version lacks vv. 22–24. Out of the seven sample versions, only the NIV renders according to the traditional Hebrew text. That text, which means "we have not perished," probably originated as a wise comment on v. 23, which specifies survival. It subsequently was wrongly taken as a correction of the similar phrase here, like the textual development in 2:21. First-plural forms do not occur in the poem until v. 40; at this stage only an individual's experience is in view. Another example of commentary intruding into the text occurs at the close of 1:19 in the Greek and Syriac versions. They add "but they did not find (any)," explaining that the search for food was unavailing (Albrektson 1963, 80).

3:28 *Yahweh*: Hebrew "he."

3:32 *Rather*: Westermann and Berlin so render.

3:36 *are what the Lord notices, doesn't he*: The NRSV, NIV, and NJB render similarly. Alternatively, one may translate as a statement: "such things the Lord has never approved" (REB; similarly NAB and NJPS).

3:37 *Who . . . commanded*: Albrektson (1963, 152–53) has interpreted in this way, taking vv. 36b and 37b as parallel in construction. He finds the blessings and curses of Deut. 28 in view, whereas in the exposition I see references to prophetic literature.

3:41 *not only*: literally "in addition to," as in Lev. 18:18 (Albrektson 1963, 154–55).

3:43 *enveloped us*: The pronoun later in the line does double duty, as the REB, NJB, and GNT judge.

3:51 *What my eyes have seen*: literally "my eye," here used by metonymy "as the medium by which the man gains knowledge of the terrible events happening around him" (Provan, following Gordis, Gottwald [1954, 14], and others). The NIV similarly has "What I see."

3:59 *You have seen*: At some point the passage moves from relating a past crisis in v. 52 to a present one. This present crisis is indicated by the imperatives *judge* in v. 59 and

Take notice in v. 63. I regard the shift as beginning in
v. 59, with the NIV "you have seen" and similarly the
NAB and GNT. Then the seeing refers to God's neutral
awareness of the crisis, as in Ps. 35:17, 22, rather than to
the positive attention envisioned in v. 63. Compare Exod.
3:7, where "hear" is also used in the same neutral sense,
as evidently here in v. 61.

3:65 *hardness*: The REB translates similarly. The Hebrew noun
seems to mean "covering," and its precise sense here is
uncertain.

4:3 *womenfolk*: The REB "the daughters of my people" is probably right in adopting the plural of the Greek and Aramaic versions. The Hebrew text has been assimilated to
the singular form that occurs frequently in the book and
nearby in vv. 6 and 10.

4:6 *punishment . . . sin*: The NJPS and NJB stand out from the
other sample English versions in referring to wrongdoing and sin rather than punishment for them. As Peake
observes, the context of suffering suggests differences in
fate rather than in its cause. The compassionate tone of
my poor people also so implies. Boase (2006, 185) notes
that the contrast in v. 9 supports a reference to punishment here.

4:7 *leaders*: "Nazirites" (GNT margin) is theoretically possible
but improbable, since no traits associated with this religious group seem to be specified in the context.

4:14 *What they were forbidden (to touch) they touched with
their clothes*: This interpretation, favored by Rudolph,
Albrektson (1963, 187), Provan, and others, refers to the
priests' becoming ritually defiled and provides the verbs
of touching in vv. 14–15 with the same subject.

4:15 Instead of two two-part lines, this stanza appears to consist
of three two-part lines.

4:16 *Yahweh himself*: literally "Yahweh's face," referring to active
presence.

4:17 *could not save us*: The NRSV and NIV render in this way; compare the NJPS "cannot." The Hebrew imperfect verb, used here, can itself have this modal sense.

4:22 *will end*: The NIV so renders. The REB has "is now complete," but the future sense of the Hebrew imperfect verbs in v. 21b and in the second half-line of v. 22a suggests that the perfect verbs here and also in v. 22b are so-called perfects of confidence (Provan). Rudolph similarly refers to them as prophetic perfects.

he will . . . no longer: The same Hebrew phrasing with the sense "no longer" in vv. 15–16 suggests this rendering (Berges), rather than "never again will you be carried into exile" (REB, similarly NJB).

5:5 *We have taskmasters*: The Hebrew verb that generally means "chase" seems here to have the weaker meaning "drive hard" that it has in Syriac (Albrektson 1963, 198).

5:6 *offered*: Five of the sample modern versions take this as a description of a past, rather than a continuing or contemporary, event. But the NJPS uses a present tense and the NRSV a perfect one.

5:10 *is burning, fever*: The English versions vary because of the uncertain meanings of the verb and noun. The NIV is similar in the first case, while the NJB and GNT have the same translation in the second.

5:12 *their hands*: Whose hands were involved, those of the underlings of v. 8 (NAB, NJPS, GNT) or of the royal officials, as the remaining sample versions render? More probably the former, as the Hebrew singular form in both places suggests. A plural would otherwise have been expected here.

5:17–18 *Here is why . . . The reason is*: Is there a forward- or backward-looking reference in v. 17? Probably the former because v. 18 seems to refer to v. 17 as the overall explanation. Six of the sample versions so judge (cf. Jer. 4:28). The NIV sees in v. 17 a reference to the preceding verses and in

v. 18 an extra reason. The literal progression from "this"
to "these things" (NIV) refers to the singular *Zion* and
the plural *jackals* (Renkema).

5:22 *but*: The sense of v. 22 in its context has been a matter of
intense debate. The debate centers on the first two Hebrew
words. Four proposals found in English versions may be
mentioned here. (1) Occasionally they are regarded as two
separate particles, "For truly" (NJPS) and "For indeed"
(NAB). It is difficult to find parallels for this interpretation, but if it is valid, the final line functions as a statement
that gives a reason for the petitions in v. 21 and the effect
is not far from rendering *but*, which finds a compound
conjunction here. (2) Another attempt to find separate
particles is represented in the NEB, which follows Ehrlich
(1914, 54): "For if thou hast utterly rejected us, then great
indeed has been thy anger against us." However, the relationship between the two half-lines is more naturally
one of synonymous parallelism than of condition and
consequence. (3) If the Hebrew represents a compound
conjunction, a popular translation is that of the NRSV,
NIV, and NJB, "unless." The rendering "Or" followed
by a question in the RSV and GNT can be justified only
as a loose paraphrase of this interpretation. This option
finds here a modifying exceptive clause. The difficulty is
that elsewhere the conjunction is used after a negative
clause, e.g., in Gen. 32:26, "I will not let you go unless you
bless me," or after a question that has the virtual force
of a negative, e.g., in Mic. 6:8, which may be literally
rendered "And what does Yahweh require of you except
to act justly . . . ?" Berges finds a negative implied here:
If Yahweh does not listen to the petition, it proves a final
rejection. (4) The best option is to translate "but" with
the KJV and REB, in line with the Latin Vulgate. Then
an adversative sense introduces a contrary and separate
statement. Hillers, followed by Berlin, similarly renders
"But instead"; we may compare Lam. 3:32, where I have

translated "Rather." Generally a negative clause precedes this usage, but not invariably so, as in Gen. 40:14 ("But"); Num. 24:22 ("yet"); and 1 Kings 20:6 ("But"). The statement here has the force of a strong protest. It fits the genre of the passage well, as I explain in the exposition, corresponding as it does to the independent statements of angry rejection found in complaint psalms.

Literature Cited

Throughout the book, commentaries are referred to only by the author's name, unless they are expressly quoted, while other literature is cited by author's name, year, and page.

Commentaries

Bergant, Dianne. 2003. *Lamentations*. Abingdon Old Testament Commentaries. Nashville: Abingdon.

Berges, Ulrich. 2002. *Klagelieder*. Herders Theologischer Kommentar zum Alten Testament. Freiburg: Herder.

Berlin, Adele. 2002. *Lamentations*. Old Testament Library. Louisville: Westminster John Knox.

Boecker, Hans J. 1985. *Klagelieder*. Zürcher Bibelkommentare. Alte Testament 21. Zürich: Theologischer Verlag.

Bracke, John M. 2000. *Jeremiah 30–52 and Lamentations*. Westminster Bible Companion. Louisville: Westminster John Knox.

Calvin, John. (1850) 1950. *Commentaries on the Book of the Prophet Jeremiah and the Lamentations*. Vol. 5. Translated by John Owen. Repr., Grand Rapids: Eerdmans.

Davidson, Robert. 1985. *Jeremiah Volume 2 and Lamentations*. Daily Study Bible. Philadelphia: Westminster Press.

Dobbs-Allsopp, F. W. 2002. *Lamentations: A Bible Commentary for Teaching and Preaching*. Interpretation. Louisville: Westminster John Knox.

Droin, Jean-Marc. 1995. *Le Livre des Lamentations: "Comment?" Une traduction et un commentaire*. La Bible, porte-Parole. Geneva: Labor et Fides.

Gerstenberger, Erhard S. 2001. *Psalms, Part 2, and Lamentations*. Forms of the Old Testament Literature 15. Grand Rapids: Eerdmans.

Gordis, Robert. 1974. *The Song of Songs and Lamentations*. Rev. ed. New York: Ktav.

Hillers, Delbert R. 1992. *Lamentations*. 2nd ed. Anchor Bible 7A. New York: Doubleday.

House, Paul R. 2004. "Lamentations." Pages 267–473, 477–79 in *Song of Songs, Lamentations*. Edited by D. Garrett and P. R. House. Word Biblical Commentary 23B. Nashville: Nelson.

Kaiser, Otto. 1992. "Klagelieder." Pages 91–198 in *Das Hohe Lied, Klagelieder, das Buch Esther*. 4th ed. Edited by H. Ringgren and O. Kaiser. Alte Testament Deutsch 16:2. Göttingen: Vandenhoeck & Ruprecht.

Keil, Carl F. (1872) 1986. *Jeremiah and Lamentations*. Translated by J. Martin. Commentary on the Old Testament 8. Repr., Grand Rapids: Eerdmans.

Kraus, Hans-Joachim. 1983. *Klagelieder (= Threni)*. Biblischer Kommentar. Altes Testament 20. Neukirchen-Vluyn: Neukircher Verlag.

Nägelsbach, C. W. Eduard. 1871. *The Lamentations of Jeremiah*. Translated and edited by W. H. Hornblower. New York: Scribner.

O'Connor, Kathleen M. 2002. *Lamentations and the Tears of the World*. Maryknoll, NY: Orbis.

Peake, Arthur S. 1911. *Jeremiah and Lamentations*. Vol. 2. Century Bible. New York: Henry Frowde.

Plöger, Otto. 1969. *Die Klagelieder*. Handbuch zum Alten Testament 1:18. 2nd ed. Tübingen: Mohr.

Provan, Iain. 1991. *Lamentations*. New Century Bible. Grand Rapids: Eerdmans.

Re'emi, S. Paul. 1984. "The Theology of Hope: A Commentary on Lamentations." Pages 73–144 in *God's People in Crisis*. Edited by R. Martin-Achard and S. P. Re'emi. International Theological Commentary. Edinburgh: Handsel.

Renkema, Johan. 1998. *Lamentations*. Translated by B. Doyle. Historical Commentary on the Old Testament. Leuven: Peeters.

Reyburn, William D. 1992. *A Handbook on Lamentations*. New York: United Bible Societies.

Rudolph, Wilhelm. 1962. *Das Buch Ruth, das Hohe Lied, die Klagelieder*. Kommentar zum Alten Testament 17:1–3. Gütersloh: Mohr.

Streane, Annesley W. 1913. *The Book of the Prophet Jeremiah, Together with the Lamentations*. 2nd ed. Cambridge Bible for Schools and Colleges 21. Cambridge: Cambridge University Press.

Weiser, Artur. 1958. "Klagelieder." Pages 39–112 in *Das Hohe Lied, Klagelieder, das Buch Esther*. Edited by H. Ringgren and A. Weiser. Das Alte Testament Deutsch 16:2. Göttingen: Vandenhoeck & Ruprecht.

Westermann, Claus. 1994. *Lamentations: Issues and Interpretation*. Translated by C. Muenchow. Minneapolis: Fortress.

Other Lamentations-Related Literature

Albertz, Rainer. 2003. *Israel in Exile: The History and Literature of the Sixth Century B.C.E.* Translated by D. Green. Studies in Biblical Literature 3. Atlanta: Society of Biblical Literature.

Albrektson, Bertil. 1963. *Studies in the Text and Theology of the Book of Lamentations with a Critical Edition of the Peshitta Text*. Lund: Gleerup.

Allen, Leslie C. 1976. *The Books of Joel, Obadiah, Jonah, and Micah*. New International Commentary on the Old Testament. Grand Rapids: Eerdmans.

Anderson, Gary A. 1991. *A Time to Mourn, a Time to Dance: The Expression of Grief and Joy in Israelite Religion*. University Park: Pennsylvania State University Press.

Barthélemy, Dominique. 1963. *Les devanciers d'Aquila.* Supplements to Vetus Testamentum 10. Leiden: Brill.

Berges, Ulrich. 2000. "'Ich bin der Mann, der Elend sah' (Klgl 3, 1): Zionstheologie als Weg aus der Krise." *Biblische Zeitschrift* 44:1–20.

Boase, Elizabeth. 2006. *The Fulfillment of Doom? The Dialogic Interaction between the Book of Lamentations and Pre-Exilic/Early Exilic Prophetic Literature.* Library of Hebrew Bible/Old Testament Studies 437. New York: T&T Clark.

Brandscheidt, Renate. 1983. *Gotteszorn und Menschenlied: Die Gerichtsklage des leidenden Gerichtung in Klagelieder 3.* Trier: Paulinus.

Broyles, Craig. 1989. *The Conflict of Faith and Experience in the Psalms: A Form-Critical and Theological Study.* Journal for the Study of the Old Testament Supplement Series 52. Sheffield: JSOT Press.

Brunet, Gilbert. 1968. *Les Lamentations contra Jérémie: Réinterpretation des quatres premières Lamentations.* Bibliothèque de l'École des Hautes Études. Section des Sciences Religieuses 75. Paris: Presses Universitaires de France.

Childs, Brevard S. 1979. *Introduction to the Old Testament as Scripture.* London: SCM Press.

Clark, Gordon R. 1993. *The Word Hesed in the Hebrew Bible.* Journal for the Study of the Old Testament Supplement Series 157. Sheffield: JSOT Press.

Cohen, Chaim. 1973. "The 'Widowed' City." *Journal of the Ancient Near Eastern Society* 5:75–81.

Dobbs-Allsopp, F. W. 1997. "Tragedy, Tradition, and Theology in the Book of Lamentations." *Journal for the Study of the Old Testament* 74:29–60.

———. 1998. "Linguistic Evidence for the Date of Lamentations." *Journal of the Ancient Near Eastern Society* 26:1–36.

———. 2004. "R(az/ais)ing Zion in Lamentations 2." Pages 21–68 in *David and Zion: Biblical Studies in Honor of J. J. M. Roberts.* Edited by B. F. Batto and K. L. Roberts. Winona Lake, IN: Eisenbrauns.

Ehrlich, Arnold. 1914. "Der Klagelieder." Pages 30–54 in *Randglossen zur hebräischen Bibel.* Vol. 7. Leipzig: Heinrichs.

Ferris, Paul W., Jr. 1992. *The Genre of Communal Lament in the Bible and the Ancient Near East*. Society of Biblical Literature Dissertation Series 127. Atlanta: Scholars Press.

Follis, Elaine R. 1987. "The Holy City as Daughter." Pages 173–84 in *Directions in Biblical Hebrew Poetry*. Edited by E. R. Follis. Journal for the Study of the Old Testament Supplement Series 40. Sheffield: JSOT Press.

Frevel, Christian. 2002. "Zerbrochene Zier: Tempel und Tempelzerstörung in den Klageliedern (Threni)." Pages 99–153 in *Gottesstadt und Gottesgarten: Zu Geschichte und Theologie des Jerusalemer Tempels*. Edited by O. Keel and E. Zenger. Quaestiones disputatae 191. Freiburg: Herder.

Gottlieb, Hans. 1978. *A Study on the Text of Lamentations*. Translated by J. Sturdy. Aarhus: Jutlandica 12:48.

Gottwald, Norman K. 1954. *Studies in the Book of Lamentations*. Studies in Biblical Theology 14. Chicago: A. R. Allenson.

———. 1993. "The Book of Lamentations Reconsidered." Pages 165–73 in *The Hebrew Bible in Its Social World and Ours*. Society of Biblical Literature Semeia Studies. Atlanta: Scholars Press.

Gous, Ignatious G. P. 1992. "Psychological Survival: Strategies in Lamentations 3 in the Light of Neuro-Linguistic Programming." Pages 317–41 in *Old Testament Science and Reality*. Edited by W. Wessels and E. Scheffler. Pretoria: Verba Vitae.

———. 1993. "Exiles and the Dynamics of Experience of Loss." *Old Testament Essays* 6:351–63.

———. 1996. "Mind over Matter: Lamentations 4 in the Light of the Cognitive Sciences." *Scandinavian Journal of the Old Testament* 10:69–87.

Heater, Homer, Jr. 1992. "Structure and Meaning in Lamentations." *Bibliotheca Sacra* 149:304–15.

Heim, Knut M. 1999. "The Personification of Jerusalem and the Drama of Her Bereavement in Lamentations." Pages 129–69 in *Zion, City of Our God*. Edited by R. S. Hess and G. J. Wenham. Grand Rapids: Eerdmans.

Hunter, Jannie. 1996. *Faces of a Lamenting City: The Development and Coherence of the Book of Lamentations*. Beiträge zur Erforschung des Alten Testaments und des antiken Judentum 39. Frankfurt: Peter Lang.

Johnson, Bo. 1985. "Form and Message in Lamentations." *Zeitschrift für die alttestamentliche Wissenschaft* 97:58–73.

Joyce, Paul. 1993. "Lamentations and the Grief Process: A Psychological Reading." *Biblical Interpretation* 1:304–20.

Knox, Ronald. 1956. *The Holy Bible*. London: Burns & Oates.

Labahn, Antje. 2002. "Trauern als Bewältigung der Vergangenheit zur Gestaltung der Zukunft: Bemerkungen zur anthropologischen Theologie der Klagelieder." *Vetus Testamentum* 52:513–27.

———. 2003. "Metaphor and Intertextuality: 'Daughter of Zion' as a Test Case." *Scandinavian Journal of the Old Testament* 17:49–67.

———. 2005. "Wild Animals and Chasing Shadows: Animal Metaphors in Lamentations as Indicators for Individual Threat." Pages 67–97 in *Metaphor in the Hebrew Bible*. Edited by P. van Hecke. Bibliotheca Ephemeridum Lovaniensium 187. Leuven: Leuven University Press.

Lee, Nancy C. 2002. *The Singers of Lamentations: Cities under Siege, from Ur to Jerusalem to Sarajevo*. Biblical Interpretation 60. Leiden: Brill.

Linafelt, Tod. 2000. *Surviving Lamentations: Catastrophe, Lament, and Protest in the Afterlife of a Biblical Book*. Chicago: University of Chicago Press.

Mintz, Alan. 1982. "The Rhetoric of Lamentations." *Prooftexts* 2:1–17.

Moore, Michael S. 1983. "Human Suffering in Lamentations." *Revue biblique* 90:534–55.

Morrow, William S. 2006. *Protest against God: The Eclipse of a Biblical Tradition*. Hebrew Bible Monographs 4. Sheffield: Sheffield Phoenix Press.

Olyan, Saul M. 2004. *Biblical Mourning: Ritual and Social Dimensions*. Oxford: Oxford University Press.

Parry, Robin. 2006. "Prolegomena to Christian Theological Interpretations of Lamentations." Pages 393–415 in *Canon and Biblical Interpretation*. Edited by C. G. Bartholomew et al. Grand Rapids: Zondervan.

Patrick, Dale. 1981. *The Rendering of God in the Old Testament*. Overtures to Biblical Theology. Philadelphia: Fortress.

Peels, Hendrik G. L. 1994. *The Vengeance of God: The Meaning of the Root NQM and the Function of the NQM-Texts in the Context of Divine Revelation in the Old Testament*. Oudtestamentische Studiën 31. Leiden: Brill.

Pham, Xuan H. T. 1999. *Mourning in the Ancient Near East and the Hebrew Bible*. Journal for the Society of the Old Testament Supplement Series 302. Sheffield: Sheffield Academic Press.

Reimer, David J. 2002. "Good Grief? A Psychological Reading of Lamentations." *Zeitschrift für die alttestamentliche Wissenschaft* 114:542–59.

Renkema, Johan. 1988. "The Literary Structure of Lamentations (I–IV)." Pages 294–396 in *The Structural Analysis of Biblical and Canaanite Poetry*. Edited by W. van der Meer and J. C. de Moor. Journal for the Society of the Old Testament Supplement Series 74. Sheffield: JSOT Press.

Salters, Robert B. 1986. "Lamentation 1.3: Light from the History of Exegesis." Pages 73–89 in *A Word in Season: Essays in Honor of William McKane*. Edited by J. D. Martin and P. R. Davies. Journal for the Study of the Old Testament Supplement Series 42. Sheffield: JSOT Press.

Schäfer, Rolf. 2006. "Der ursprüngliche Text und die poetische Struktur des ersten Klageliedes (Klg 1): Textkritik und Strukturanalyse in Zwiegespräch." Pages 239–59 in *Sôfer Mahîr: Essays in Honor of Adrian Schenker Offered by Editors of Biblia Hebraica Quinta*. Edited by Y. A. P. Goldman, A. van der Kooij, and R. D. Weis. Supplements to Vetus Testamentum 110. Leiden: Brill.

Tov, Emanuel. 2001. *Textual Criticism of the Hebrew Bible*. 2nd ed. Minneapolis: Fortress.

Westermann, Claus. 1998. "The Complaint against God." Translated by A. Siedlecki. Pages 233–41 in *God in the Fray: A Tribute to Walter Brueggemann*. Edited by T. Linafelt and T. K. Beal. Minneapolis: Fortress.

Wiesmann, Hermann. 1926. "Der planmässige Aufbau der Klagelieder des Jeremias." *Biblica* 7:146–61.

Yadin, Yigael. 1963. *The Art of Warfare in Biblical Lands*. 2 vols. New York: McGraw-Hill.

Grief Biographies

Barkin, Carol, et al. 2004. *Beyond Tears: Living after Losing a Child*. New York: St. Martin's Press.

Bridger, Francis. 2004. *23 Days: A Story of Love, Death, and God*. London: Darton, Longman & Todd.

Brooks, Anne M. 1985. *The Grieving Time: A Year's Account of Recovery from Loss*. Garden City, NY: Dial Press.

Brothers, Joyce. 1990. *Widowed*. New York: Ballantine.

Broyard, Sandy. 2005. *Standby*. New York: Knopf.

Caine, Lynn. 1974. *Widow*. New York: Morrow.

Carter, Abigail. 2008. *The Alchemy of Loss: A Young Widow's Transformation*. Deerfield Beach, FL: Health Communications.

Claypool, John. 2006. "What Can We Expect of God?" Pages 33–51 in *This Incomplete One: Words Occasioned by the Death of a Young Person*. Edited by M. D. Bush. Grand Rapids: Eerdmans.

Didion, Joan. 2006. *The Year of Magical Thinking*. New York: Vintage.

Edington, J. Howard. 2006. "When the Waters Are Deep." Pages 67–78 in *This Incomplete One: Words Occasioned by the Death of a Young Person*. Edited by M. D. Bush. Grand Rapids: Eerdmans.

Erdal, Jennie. 2005. *Ghosting: A Double Life*. New York: Doubleday.

Frankl, Viktor E. 1963. *Man's Search for Meaning: An Introduction to Logotherapy*. Rev. ed. Translated by I. Lasch. New York: Washington Square.

Fumia, Molly. 2000. *A Piece of My Heart: Living through the Grief of Miscarriage, Stillbirth, or Infant Death*. Berkeley, CA: Conari Press.

Hood, Ann. 2008. *Comfort: A Journey through Grief*. New York: Norton.

Irish, Jerry A. 1975. *A Boy Thirteen: Reflections on Death*. Philadelphia: Westminster Press.

Korobkin, Frieda S. 2008. *Throw Your Feet over Your Shoulders: Beyond the Kindertransport*. New York: Devora.

Lewis, C. S. (1961) 1976. *A Grief Observed*, with an Afterword by Chad Walsh. Repr., New York: Bantam.

Newlin, Jeffrey. 2006. "Standing at the Grave." Pages 119–30 in *This Incomplete One: Words Occasioned by the Death of a Young Person*. Edited by M. D. Bush. Grand Rapids: Eerdmans.

Nouwen, Henri. 1982. *A Letter of Consolation*. San Francisco: Harper & Row.

Schleiermacher, Friedrich. 2006. "Sermon at Nathanael's Grave." Pages 145–53 in *This Incomplete One: Words Occasioned by the Death of a Young Person*. Edited by M. D. Bush. Grand Rapids: Eerdmans.

Sittser, Gerald. 1996. *A Grace Disguised: How the Soul Grows through Loss*. Grand Rapids: Zondervan.

Weems, Ann. 1995. *Psalms of Lament*, with a foreword by Walter Brueggemann. Louisville: Westminster John Knox.

Wiesel, Elie. 1995. *All Rivers Run to the Sea: Memories*. New York: Knopf.

Wolterstorff, Nicholas. 1987. *Lament for a Son*. Grand Rapids: Eerdmans.

Other Grief Literature

Alcoholics Anonymous. 2001. 4th ed. New York: Alcoholics Anonymous World Services, Inc. Also known as *The Big Book*.

Archer, John. 1999. *The Nature of Grief: The Evolution and Psychology of Reactions to Loss*. London: Routledge.

Bouvard, Marguerite, and Evelyn Gnadu. 1998. *The Path through Grief: A Compassionate Guide*. Amherst, NY: Prometheus.

Daniels, Linda. 2004. *Healing Journeys: How Trauma Survivors Learn to Live Again*. Far Hills, NJ: New Horizon Press.

Gravitz, Herbert L., and Julie D. Bowden. 1987. *Recovery: A Guide for Adult Children of Alcoholics*. New York: Simon & Schuster.

Jung, Carl G. 1954. *The Practice of Psychotherapy: Essays on the Psychology of the Transference and Other Subjects*. Translated by R. F. C.

Hull. Vol. 16 of *The Collected Works of C. G. Jung*. New York: Pantheon.

Kübler-Ross, Elisabeth, and David Kessler. 2005. *On Grief and Grieving: Finding the Meaning of Grief through the Five Stages of Loss*. New York: Scribner.

Lester, Andrew D. 1995. *Hope in Pastoral Care and Counseling*. Louisville: Westminster John Knox.

Lord, Janice H. 1990. *No Time for Goodbyes: Coping with Sorrow, Anger, and Injustice after a Tragic Death*. Ventura, CA: Pathfinder.

Maciejewski, Paul K., Baohui Zhang, Susan D. Block, and Holly G. Prigerson. 2007. "An Empirical Examination of the Stage Theory of Grief." *Journal of the American Medical Association* 297 (7):716–23.

Mitchell, Kenneth R., and Herbert Anderson. 1983. *All Our Losses, All Our Griefs: Resources for Pastoral Care*. Philadelphia: Westminster Press.

Muslin, Hyman L. 1984. "On Empathic Reading." Pages 301–16 in *Empathy*. Vol. 1. Edited by J. Lichtenberg, M. Bornstein, and D. Silver. Hillsdale, NJ: Analytic Press.

Nouwen, Henri. 1972. *The Wounded Healer: Ministry in Contemporary Society*. Garden City, NY: Doubleday.

Rando, Therese. A. 1984. *Grief, Dying, and Death: Clinical Interventions for Caregivers*. Champaign, IL: Research Press.

———. 1993. *Treatment of Complicated Mourning*. Champaign, IL: Research Press.

Sanders, Catherine M. 1999. *Grief: The Mourning After: Dealing with Adult Bereavement*. 2nd ed. New York: Wiley.

Soelle, Dorothee. 1975. *Suffering*. Translated by E. Kalin. Philadelphia: Fortress.

Wilcox, Danny M. 1998. *Alcoholic Thinking: Language, Culture, and Belief in Alcoholics Anonymous*. Westport, CT: Praeger.

Zinner, Ellen S., and Mary B. Williams, eds. 1999. *When a Community Weeps: Case Studies in Group Survivorship*. Philadelphia: Brunner/Mazel.

Miscellaneous

Drapkin, Jennifer, and Sarah Zielinski. 2009. "Celestial Sleuth." *Smithsonian* 40 (1): 70–75.

Jones, Michael. 2008. *Leningrad: State of Siege*. New York: Basic Books.

Lawler, Andrew. 2009. "Iran's Hidden Jewel." *Smithsonian* 40 (1): 36–46.

Niebuhr, Reinhold. 1964. "The Religion of Abraham Lincoln." Pages 72–87 in *Lincoln and the Gettysburg Address: Commemorative Papers*. Edited by A. Nevins. Urbana: University of Illinois Press.

Wilcox, Ellen Wheeler. 1958. *One Hundred and One Famous Poems*. Rev. ed. Edited by R. J. Cook. Chicago: Reilly and Lee.

Scripture Index